What pe

According to the adage, parapł
makes us stronger," Michael Ga
What he has lived through has made him a stronger writer and left him with
some profound lessons to share.

–DON MCLEESE – University of Iowa journalism professor and veteran music
and culture critic for the *Chicago Sun-Times*, the *Austin American-Statesman*,
and *Rolling Stone*.

Michael is a rare combination of philosopher and storyteller. His book *Waking Up*
was exactly what I needed to make a lasting change in my life.

–ADAM CARROLL – Speaker, entrepreneur, and host of the *Build A Bigger
Life* Podcast

I am so appreciative of this book and the absolute perfect timing of it. This will be
my Christmas gift for all my loved ones, this book can change your life and I am
so GRATEFUL that you shared it with me!

–TRINA B.

It is rare to come across a book that is as genuine and entertaining as this one.
Topics like addiction and mental health can be sensitive to discuss but the way
Michael candidly shares what he went through makes his story extremely relat-
able. That kind of vulnerability is at the heart of what makes us all human.

–SHAWN CAROLAN – American Airlines

This book was so impactful for me. I read it cover to cover in one day. I could
not put it down. The vulnerability and honest story telling causes an immediate
connection. I cried, several times to be honest, I laughed out loud and scared the
people around me at the airport, I found many useful suggestions that I could
immediately implement. Thank you for putting this out there. My hope is that it
will resonate with many others as much as it did with me.

–MATT B.

Help Your Organization to Wake Up!

Do you have an event coming up that requires a dynamic
public speaker or corporate coaching?
Speaking and coaching engagements with Michael
Gallagher can be arranged through
his website at
www.michaelgallagherspeaks.com

Catch up with Michael J Gallagher and check out extra
content not included in this book. Visit him at
www.wakingupthebook.com

A portion of the author's proceeds for this book will benefit
Creative Visions. Their beautiful vision is to break the chain
of poverty and hopelessness within vulnerable communities
Visit them at www.cvonline.us

A Note from David Meltzer

David Meltzer is a 3x bestselling author and Co-founder of Sports 1 Marketing with his business partner Hall of Fame Quarterback Warren Moon. He formerly served as CEO of the renowned Leigh Steinberg Sports & Entertainment agency, which was the inspiration for the movie Jerry Maguire. His life's mission is to empower OVER 1 BILLION people to be happy!

The universe tends to give you a touch of favor when you are least expecting it. That is certainly true for me, as I met Michael through a text message. It came through on a Monday evening and said, "Hi Dave. I wanted to say thank you for sharing your story about going bankrupt and especially how ego was involved. I loved what you had to say about radical humility!"

In the content I put out, I often tell my story about making my first million dollars less than nine months from graduation from law school, and how I continued to build wealth until I had a net worth of over $100 million. I also share how I ended up losing it all and then earned it all back, while committing to my new mission in life, to empower over 1 billion people to be happy. It was during one of my speaking engagements that Michael had received my number, and after that text message I invited Michael to join me in my private coaching group and he accepted. Since then, Michael and I had a lot of fun and have learned an immense amount, so when he asked me to write a few words as an opening for this book, I jumped at the chance.

As you read Michael's early story it may seem at times sad, but what you will hear over and over is that he is grateful for his experiences. That is exactly why the message in this book is such a powerful one. The lesson of gratitude is one of the first lessons we learn in life, to say thank you, and it is also one of the most valuable. Saying thank you is such a simple thing, but to develop gratitude changes lives dramatically.

When I speak to people all over the world, on TV shows, in my books, and on podcasts, one of my favorite pieces of advice is "If you want to completely change your life, say thank you before you go to bed and thank you when you wake up every single day." By viewing life through the lens of gratitude, we are able to see the light, the love and the lessons in everything that we experience.

As you read this book, and hear its message, I think you will see that lesson applied over and over.

David Meltzer

Co-founder of Sports 1 Marketing,
best-selling author, and top business coach

WAKING UP
UP

A GUIDE FOR TRANSFORMATION

MICHAEL J GALLAGHER

Disclaimer

This book is not intended as a substitute for the medical advice of physicians and/or mental health professionals. The reader should regularly consult a physician and/or mental health professional in matters relating to his/her health and particularly with respect to any symptoms that may require diagnosis or treatment of medical or psychological concerns.
Some names and identifying details have been changed to protect the privacy of individuals

To request permissions, contact the publisher at
info@wakingupthebook.com

ISBN
Paperback: 978-0-578-76014-8

First edition September 2020

Edited by Shawnna Stiver / shawnna@kindco.org
Cover art by Micah Marquez / 100 Covers
Layout by Dragan Bilic / draganbilic@yahoo.com
Photography by Chelsy Zimmerman / poppyphotographybychelsy.me

For my house full of strong women,

Michaelle, Gabby, Emma, Mary, and Mabel,

you are amazing!

Acknowledgments

Writing a book is harder than I thought and more rewarding than I could have imagined. I'd like to thank a few people for the support they have given me:

My mom and dad, Sharon and Jerry Gallagher, who were both beautiful people and did the best that they could.

My wife, Michaelle, who put up with my obsession and seeming inability to talk about anything else while I was writing this. Thank you Michaelle, for your compassion and strength through the difficult years, and for being a rock for our family. Without you, I may never have woken up.

My daughters, Gabrielle, Emma, Mary and Mabel, you amaze me each and every day by reminding me to be curious and to have fun. Thank you for teaching me to be a better person. I love you more than all the stars in the sky.

Jeff and Dee Dolton who made me a part of their family. Thank you Jeff and Dee, I love you.

My cousin Carrie Black who inspired me with her courage and whose pragmatism always made me smile. I miss you Carrie.

Shawnna Stiver, my editor who taught me the word misophonia and helped me make a book out of something that wasn't. Thank you, Shawnna, your encouragement when I had moments of doubt was amazing! This is pretty F'n cool!

Don McLeese, who kindly encouraged me and helped this along. Thank you, Don.

Adam Carroll, who always makes others feel good when they are with him. Thank you, Adam, for laughing at my off-color stories and reminding me that being curious about other people is a reward in itself.

David Meltzer, a coach, mentor, and exceedingly kind human being. Thank you, David.

Scribe Book School who provide an unbelievable amount of content for writers.

All of the friends I found within Recovery Dharma.

Peter Pintus, one of the most compassionate men I have ever known.

And my friend, Andrew, for our many long talks. I love you brother.

Contents

Introduction

You Have Already Won the Lottery

I was standing in a dirty bedroom; the bed was unmade with a nasty looking blanket crumpled on it. There were boxes of junk sitting around. The worn-out carpet was filthy; it smelled like stale smoke and the dim light bulb in the fixture made the room feel small and dismal. I could hear people talking in the other room a few feet away, but I couldn't make out what they were saying because I couldn't take my eyes off the sawed-off shotgun pointed at my chest.

"Why the fuck you bring that white boy to my fuckin' house mother fucker?"

It wasn't the first time that I had a gun pointed at me, but this time I thought I was going to die. Butch, the old guy I had been buying my crack from, was high, paranoid and pissed!

Thankfully that scene and that life is my past, and I say, thankfully, not just because it's over but because of what it gave me. Fast forward to today. I'm clean and sober. This morning I awoke early, as is my habit. I read, I meditated, and I exercised. I am present. I am living my dream life: my daughter Mabel and I ate breakfast together, we talked about the dreams she had overnight, where kittens with superpowers moved in with us and became friends with Magnus, our overweight cat. With her sitting in my lap excitedly telling me the magic of a 5-year-old's mind, my beautiful wife walked into the room and gave us both a hug.

We get to live in a nice home, travel extensively, and have the luxury to spend time with our children. Today I'm an avid reader and learner and I'm teaching myself a third language (my goal is five). I have a purpose each day, the autonomy to grow, a sense of worth, but more than anything else, I am happy. Truly happy.

How did my life change from addiction, depression, desperation, and hopelessness, to one of gratitude, compassion, creativity, and inner peace? I found tools to get there. It took me a very long time. But it doesn't have to take a long time. The truth is that once I believed it could change, change came very quickly. I want to share how to, not only solve massive problems like alcoholism and drug addiction, but also give you the tools to overcome other limiting beliefs and behaviors, whatever they are for you. Also, to teach you to not just overcome them, but to go far beyond that to a life of abundance, love, compassion, and happiness. You'll learn to chart your own course, build your vision and believe you will get there. You'll smash your goals and go way above them. And finally, you'll learn how to live your dream life and help other people at the same time.

When I map out any project, I think of it as having big blocks, then smaller blocks and then even smaller blocks that need to be accomplished in order to get a desirable outcome. For example, to help my 5-year-old daughter clean her messy room, I cannot fire off 20 things for her to do. It is overwhelming, a 5-year-old doesn't have the attention span for that, and frankly, neither do I.

So, I might start with one big block: "First, make your bed." That's a good foundation.

"Second, pick up all of your toys and put them in your toy box."

After she finishes this, I tell her, "Now pick up all of the clothes that are on your floor and put them in a pile on your bed."

Just those three blocks make an enormous difference in her room. Then we get into a few smaller blocks.

"Now sort the clothes into two piles: clean and dirty." I don't know if your kids do this, but mine throw three things on the floor for each item they actually wear."

"Now fold the clean clothes, put them away and place the dirty clothes in the hamper."

Then we move on to stuff like straightening dressers, dusting, etc. You get the point.

This book contains what I think of as the big blocks of change. The method I personally used to transform my life. This is how I changed my thinking to go from where I began to where I am. It's a way of changing thought patterns and habits. Just like when my daughter cleans her room, there is room for her to move on to the smaller blocks and then to refine it even further. But these big blocks are a starting point. And I'll let you in on a secret: with the big blocks in place, the rest flows naturally.

What is it you want to change? Do you want happier relationships, to travel, wealth, freedom to make a difference in the world, more time with your family, to be at peace, or to simply be a compassionate human being?

Truly, at the root of all those things is simply the desire that we all have: to be happy. If you have a desire not only to change but to transform, I invite you to read my story, consider the tools I used, and if they make sense to you, put them into practice.

You are so much more than perhaps you now believe. You have greatness inside of you, untapped resources and depths of compassion. I tell you this with the utmost sincerity and without a single, solitary doubt. I can say this because I have experienced it and I am no more special than you. I am one ordinary human out of 7.5 billion humans on our planet, with mostly the same qualities that everyone else has. I wasn't born into a wealthy family; I don't have an Ivy League education. The biggest difference is that I have been lucky enough to live a life with circumstances that FORCED me to wake up. Every day I am grateful for it!

What I came to realize is that most people are walking around in a mass hallucination, living with habits born from fear and beliefs that keep them asleep from their true potential. Contrary to the nature of what they really are, they exist, breathe and die, and never really live.

Take a moment to consider the incredible odds against existing at all. For you to exist, many events had to take place precisely as they did. Did you know that the odds of the exact same sperm and egg that encoded your DNA meeting and making you are 250 million to one? And this incredible phenomenon had to happen the same way millions of times for the generations of your genetic ancestors before you. With each one overcoming the same odds. This is just one part of it. Think for a moment of the odds that the earth was formed and is habitable, that our solar system and then our planet became a place that would not only support life, but that life would take hold and flourish. When we look at it that way, each of us has already won the lottery!

Call it chance, luck, a divine source, the universe, Allah, God or whatever your personal belief is, something has already overcome the greatest of odds *for you* and placed you here. You are aware and conscious. It's as if the universe is conspiring to make you successful. What will *you* do with it? Far too many people reach the end of their lives and regret how they have lived. I imagine they feel their lives were short. You don't have to feel that way. You have the choice!

The Roman Stoic Seneca said it much better than I can when he wrote: *It is not that we have a short space of time, but that we waste much of it. Life is long enough, and it has been given in sufficiently generous measure to allow the accomplishment of the very greatest things if the whole of it is well invested. But when it is squandered in luxury and carelessness, when it is devoted to no good end, forced at last by the ultimate necessity we perceive that it has passed away before we were aware that it was passing. So it is—the life we receive is not short, but we make it so, nor do we have any lack of it, but are wasteful of it.*[1]

Wow!

As my father was getting on in years, he said something similar, albeit not so eloquent. He lived a checkered life that I will tell you about. He had suffered a severe back injury and as he aged it left him in constant pain. So, I was often concerned, and I would ask, "How are you today Pop?" His response was always the same. He would say: "Nobody threw dirt on me after I fell asleep last night, I must be doing pretty well." In other words, if he woke up in the morning and was alive, regardless of his challenges, he had great opportunity and would live accordingly. How many of the "important things" that we concentrate on, become a lot less important if we live with that viewpoint?

So, if nobody threw dirt on you after you fell asleep last night, I challenge you to wake up! Don't be content with simply existing. Our lives can "*allow the accomplishment of the very greatest things.*" Use your mind, body and spirit to take advantage of the most precious opportunity you have. To really live! I implore you to believe that you can. After all, you have all of the luck in the universe; it is conspiring to make you successful and you have already won the lottery!

Here is some of my story.

---

1   Seneca, Lucius Annaeus, and Moses Hadas. *The Stoic Philosophy of Seneca: Essays and Letters of Seneca.* New York: W.W. Norton and Company, 1968.

One

Who Should We Choose as Our Heroes?

My cheap cell phone jingled in my left pants pocket. I half apologized to the woman sitting across the desk who was looking sternly at me as I flipped it open to my brother Gary's voice. "Michael?" he asked. "Yeah what's up I'm in the middle of something?" I replied. I'm not sure if he could hear the irritation in my voice. I was edgy because I was without any cocaine and I hadn't had a drink yet that day. The something I was in the middle of was answering questions asked by the intake nurse where I was checking myself into rehab. My family didn't know where I was. I was running. I seemed to be out of options. I couldn't see a light at the end of this tunnel. I didn't actually want to get clean, but I thought I could use rehab to just slow down for a little while.

"They just took dad to the emergency room. You need to meet us there," Gary told me. my dad going to the emergency room wasn't the scary part of that sentence. It was the "You need to meet us there." My mind began to race with fear. If it weren't serious, I wouldn't be summoned. Not only was I disfellowshipped—or in other words, excommunicated from my family's religion—I had become more and more unreliable in almost every way in my life. My family had long since stopped including me in information or expectation. "Where?" Was the only word that came out. He told me and as I hung up I half apologetically excused myself from the not so surprised nurse. Selfishly I thought I had received a reprieve and headed across town.

On the ride over, my mind went to another time we got bad news about my dad. I stood shirtless and barefoot in the middle of the street wearing an old pair of jeans beside my brother Gary watching my mother and two older brothers drive away. It was a summer evening, the sun was setting bright orange and pink across the sky and the air carried the smell of asphalt that had been laid nearby. The locusts were tuning up in the background for their mournful drone. Somewhere maybe other kids were being called to dinner or perhaps still out playing catch with their dad. At eight years old, I already knew I wasn't like them and that our family was different.

As the car turned the corner out of my view, tears tracked down my dirty face and my skinny little body began to shake and sob as Gary put his arm around my shoulders. Just a little while earlier my three brothers and I were camped out in the living room of our dumpy trailer house watching TV.

My mom was in the kitchen preparing dinner. I don't recall what we had been watching but the memory of what happened next is still frozen in my mind. The local news flashed a picture of my father's face. It was an old mug shot.

"According to the police department, the alleged armed robber Gerald Steele Gallagher, suffered a gunshot wound in the incident. His condition is unknown," the newscaster relayed.

I began to feel separate from my body. There was a bustle of activity and excitement around me that I was not a part of. I was floating somewhere away from it and felt off to the side. I recall my mom retreating to a neighbor's house to use the phone and a little while later returning. She told me, as if speaking to an adult, "Your dad has been shot. They don't know if he will live. You're going to go to the neighbors down the road while I go to the hospital."

I cried and begged because I wanted to go with her. But only Mark and Paul, my two older brothers would be going. Gary, who was only two years older than me, and I would have to stay away. I just wanted to see my dad. To know he was ok. To have him say, "Well halloo Michael J," drawing out the words to make them sound warm and loving just like he always did. To show me his smile that somehow seemed to well up a sense of security in me.

I have long seen my father as a dichotomy of character between gentle and kind to me to another side of violence seemingly without remorse to the world outside our family. When I was a child, he seemed larger than life. He always had a smile on his face when I caught his glance. He was loving and kind, ready to give me a hug or say something funny that would make me feel safe. He'd wrap his prison tattoo-covered arms around me and pick me up squeezing me in a hug with an almost benevolent light in his eyes. I had heard the stories about him though, mostly from my older brothers, who in turn had heard them from my dad's associates. We never heard the stories from our father. There was the time he had beaten a man in prison with a metal mop bucket wringer to the point of almost killing him over a stolen candy bar. Or the time someone hadn't paid what he was owed and so he smashed his teeth on a concrete curb, and someone else he had shot in Kansas City in an altercation. Even as a little kid I think I picked up on how tense outsiders were when they were around my dad. (Maybe like the feeling I get when I'm in a house or yard with a large dog I'm not sure about). I could sense their uneasiness. For the most part I think my dad kept his violent nature away from our home and family when he could. I remember only a couple of times seeing the switch flipped, and it was as if he were a different person altogether. When I was six I witnessed him pull a convenience store clerk over the counter and beat him unconscious over an argument about his Pepsi. He tapped into anger like a dynamo and it took on a life of its own.

This was the same man who when I would get stuck after climbing a tree too high, becoming paralyzed with fear, would make the climb himself, put me on his back and carry me to safety. No matter how many times it happened, he was still kind and patient, assuaging my tears with his tenderness. There were many examples like this. It's difficult for a son to put those two sides next to one another and make them add up, to know which to choose as the hero.

My dad had been dealing with congestive heart failure for a few years and had lived through several heart attacks. The morning my brother Gary called me, my dad had gotten out of bed, walked on his own to the living room and told my mom he wasn't feeling well. He sat down on the couch and a little while later went by ambulance to the hospital. By the time I reached him, he was in the emergency room connected to a heart monitor and had an oxygen mask on. I don't recall that he was alert but I remember taking his hand in mine. Even as an adult, his giant hand dwarfed my own. As I stood there holding his hand it felt warm ... until it wasn't.

The next day I showed up to meet two of my brothers at the funeral home where our dad was to be cremated. The man asked if we wanted to see him one last time. Both of my brothers said no. Maybe it was me being dramatic and the *I need for you to see how sad I am* person in me that made me say yes. Or maybe it was the fact that they had progressively said their goodbyes to him while I was absent, bouncing from one party to another and then from one drug house to another. As I look back, my absence is one of many examples of how I selfishly took something from other people to quiet the continuous noise in my head.

I walked down a hallway, lit only by the sunlight from outside, around a corner and into a room that smelled like antiseptic and cut flowers. *Why weren't the fucking lights on?* I raged in my head. In the dim room his body lay covered. I moved the sheet and looked at his face, it was dull, not him. His strong arms were limp beside him.

Again, memory took me to an earlier time. It was shortly before he was shot. We were living in the same hopeless trailer court. I stood in the hallway but could see through the kitchen into the front of the trailer where my parent's bed was. He was in bed, my mom sat beside him with a bowl of water and a washcloth dabbing his forehead. "I just can't get warm," I heard him say. Even though he was under a pile of blankets and sweating. He shook uncontrollably. Even at my young age I understood that he was coming down off something, or maybe trying to kick it again. Out of concern, my older brother Paul took me aside. He didn't have reassuring words. That wasn't our way. Instead he was trying to prepare me. At 14, he had already become a grown up in most ways, living from one type of chaos to the next. He understood what was going on. "Dad is detoxing. You need to stay away from him right now. One of his friends died this way." That sentence burned into my brain: "One of his friends died this way." I don't remember how long the detox took I only remember the fear.

It seems he didn't clean up for long. We were riding in his pickup a few months later but he wasn't with us. My mom was driving and my brothers and I were squeezed into the single row seat coming home from the church late in the evening. The seat was a dirty cloth and vinyl with a tear across the backrest where I always placed my little hand and picked at the cotton stuffing. This time I felt something that wasn't stuffing. It was a plastic crinkly package. I crunched the package a few times between my fingers trying to figure out what it was and then pulled it out and asked, "What's this?" My mom snatched my dad's package of syringes from my hand, her face becoming angry. My parents fought late into the night as I lay in bed believing it was my fault.

The body in front of me now looked cold and gray. Even the faded tattoo of a cross and little flowers with the words "In Memory of Mother" covering his left arm looked dead. It wasn't him lying there. A primal knowing of sorts peeked through at me. It's happened a few times since when I've been with loved ones after death. Even after the experience with my dad, I would still go through years of differing beliefs, several of them were resolute atheism. But that pinprick feeling or "knowing," where one moment the person I knew and loved was there and the next they were gone, would resurface, become immense and eventually wake me up.

Being an addict and alcoholic, it's not hard to imagine what I did next. I had to get rid of it. I had to bury it. This terrible way I felt. The thoughts and feelings of loss that wouldn't stop invading every single moment. The exact memory of *where* I went next and with *whom* is dull because those details weren't important to me. I was on a barstool somewhere with bourbon in a glass, no rocks. I remember *that* vividly, the ceremony of the thick medicine-like syrup pouring from bottle to glass and then finally into my mouth. The warm feeling it gave me was like being a child wrapped in a blanket standing atop a furnace vent with the warm air enveloping me. I craved the love and security it provided, and mostly the quiet it brought to my mind. And as I sat there grappling with the loss of the man who had been my confusing hero, I thought of him as this unattainable epitome of what a man should be: one who had come from a childhood of terrible abuse but still showed love to his children. He had survived countless brawls, drug addiction, even being shot in the head, and spent most of my childhood behind bars, but ultimately remained clean and sober for 18 years. This man, built in shades of grey that I couldn't fit into my black and white brain, easily faded as I tilted my glass one more time.

Two

God, Murder, and Zombies

In trying to give a sense of who my mom was, I continue to fail. It's as if I'm looking at an old black and white photograph of a person I know but from a time before I knew them. I can write a description, but I can't get a grasp of who she actually was. When I examine the reason for this, I come to what must be only one of a few conclusions and all of them leave me with disquieting thoughts.

The personality of the woman I knew was inexorably meshed with her religion, which seemed to steal her real personality. That, or she had little to begin with, but being her offspring, this is a difficult pill for me to swallow. It is distasteful for the same reason parents who are divorced should never make a child feel the opposite parent is worthless. It is in effect telling the child that he or she is half worthless also. Being raised with no sisters and in a restrictive religious culture that gave little access to becoming platonic friends with the opposite sex, women seem to be unknowable creatures to me. So perhaps she, like all women was simply a mystery. Something I have no understanding of, holding something back, for reasons she kept only to herself, or at least reasons I cannot understand. I prefer to think this rather than to think she had lost completely her own personality. Instead I like to imagine she held a portion of it separate and tucked away somewhere safe from what the confines of a cult allowed her to show.

So, after many attempts, I have resigned myself to describe just a few bits of my mom's personality but mostly tell you about her religion. Because it, I know too well. And describing it serves better than describing her for the purpose of painting a picture of what shaped me into an addict and alcoholic.

Sharon Gallagher had a different kind of childhood compared with the time she grew up in. Where we often see the Ozzy and Harriet ideal of post WW II for American families, this was most certainly not her experience. Her own mother, probably suffering from mental or emotional illness, abandoned her first four children (my mom and her first three siblings). This happened when my mom was just a toddler while my grandfather was away from home serving in the Navy during WWII. My grandfather eventually remarried the woman I thought of as my grandma. Her name was Margaret. My grandmother Marie married and divorced several more times. Eventually my mom had 17 full, half and stepsiblings, 23 if you count the six step-children from Marie's final marriage. Without charts, graphs and a slide rule, I don't think I can explain the family tree and how that happened. I am quite certain though that this early upheaval in her family and abandonment by her mother left her with an unfilled need for stability and love. This was one of the factors that led my mom to accept the teachings of a cult.

Yet despite the example of her own mother's abandonment mental and emotional issues and lack of loyalty to any one marriage and resulting family, my mom was one of the most loyal people I have ever known. Sometimes this was misplaced; I think of it as an example of how our greatest strength can also be our greatest weakness. When I look back on what she did, I think of her with love for the fact that through all the chaos she was always there. She was always a hard worker who taught us her work ethic and who made clear how much she loved us. Many faults and failings can be overlooked by adult children when those things are in place. My mom could have easily used drugs and alcohol to escape as my father did, and as I did, or she could have left as her own mother did, but she did not. She is a good example of doing her best with what she was given. This gave us a sense of stability that many kids never get. It was the stability she never received herself.

My parents met in their teens somewhere around 1958 and married 10 years later in 1968. Their marriage was one that contained two people with quite different lifestyles, but at their core and through a great deal of dysfunction, they loved each other deeply and remained together. As drugs and alcohol became a coping mechanism for me, religion became my mother's. About nine months after I was born in 1971, my mom was approached by a neighbor offering a free bible study course. The bible study course led to her adoption of a belief system and practice with a high mind control group: as a Jehovah's Witnesses. Today I call it a cult and not without reason, they check each of the boxes in Robert J Lifton's eight criteria of thought reform[1] (brainwashing, mind control). Here's a synopsis of their basic dogma:

We are living in what the Bible calls the last days and very soon Armageddon will begin, and any non-believers will be murdered by God's own hand.

144,000 people have the hope to go to heaven. A number it seems that has largely been filled, with the exception of the Governing Body, (The men who run the Watchtower organization), and a few others.

For the rest of the believers, their hope is to survive Armageddon to turn the planet into a physical paradise again where everyone will live forever.

Just before Armageddon though, all of the world governments led by Satan and his minions will be allowed by God to attack his chosen people (Jehovah's Witnesses) so they can prove their faith one last time before being allowed into the paradise.

---

1   Lifton, Robert Jay. *Thought Reform and the Psychology of Totalism.* London: Pelican Books, 1967.

This attack will come in the form of persecution, arrest, and torture to break the faith of God's people by the government.

Any of God's people who stay loyal will look forward to the paradise where everyone they have ever loved and lost in death will be brought back to life by God to live there with them.[2]

Except for all of the murder by God, violence, torture and zombies it doesn't sound too bad so far does it? The rule is that you need to belong to their group and live with their approval to be saved. And you will be asked to do and give more and more of yourself along the way because God also has an attendance and work policy. You are required to attend five meetings a week as well as Saturday mornings, and spend part of Sunday knocking on your neighbor's doors to save them before Armageddon. Every day personal "study" or "self-indoctrination" from the organization's books is also necessary, along with a weekly "family study" or "family indoctrination."

There is also a fraternization policy. The often-quoted Bible verse is 1 Corinthians 15:33: *Bad associations spoil useful habits.* Based on how the rules are structured, you become socially isolated. As a child it meant that you shouldn't play with the neighbor kids if they don't belong to the group. You also couldn't be involved in any organized sports at school or otherwise. Birthdays, and generally anything a kid may consider awesome, is a sin. The religion also teaches that all

---

2   Bible, English 1961. *New World Translation of the Holy Scriptures.* New York: Watchtower Bible and Tract Society, 1961.

holidays have pagan origins that make them unwholesome and sinful. Again, these are not just beliefs based on scripture. I believe they are, by design, created to socially and psychologically isolate people.

As an adult you may work anywhere, however, any career goals should align with the belief that this world is soon to end, so you need only earn the bare minimum to survive and carry on in the door-to-door ministry work. Education beyond high school is greatly frowned upon, with the possible exception of a trade school. You should remain socially distant from other students or your workmates. You live under a microscopic scrutiny of your habits and actions by the Jehovah's Witnesses group. But to ever stand up to the constant scrutiny and social isolation and say, "This is wrong!" is almost impossible because of the belief that there is absolutely nowhere else to go that won't end in death. It is also taught that to question the teachings is what the Bible calls an unforgivable sin, and someone doing so would be labeled an apostate. Even many years later as I write this, I am aware that I will be labeled as such. This feeling of having no voice, and nowhere else to go without the penalty of death from God, and the constant training to not question beliefs, results in a mental state with few limits on self-destructive behaviors in the minds and actions of Jehovah's Witnesses who either leave or are ousted by the church. If a person is fortunate enough to find their way out, alcoholism, drug use, falling prey to a different form of mind control, and or long-term emotional illness is quite common. Admitting to myself

I could no longer live under that religion's control while still harboring the underpinned belief that I would die any day at God's own hand removed almost every limit that otherwise may have reigned in my self-numbing behaviors.

These are just a few of the numerous beliefs, teachings and rules. The Watchtower has printed literally hundreds of different books and pamphlets to 'educate' their following. These teachings are designed to make a person feel different and separate from others who are not of the same faith and to hold them captive within the confines of the organization's grasp. It is a classic form of mind control.

For our family, it became a world where everything was either controlled by the rules or by the extreme culture. Fear was continuously used as a motivator. And shame was used as a punishment. It's an environment where a person loses a sense of self and children are not able to develop in a normal way. Every part of life revolves around the faith. Because every large and small part of your life decisions and actions are wrapped up in it. I'm sure I could write a volume of the big, small, significant and insignificant ways the group controlled our intellectual, emotional and physical lives. But this one story paints the picture well of how controlled our lives were, down to every intimate detail.

My father had been in prison for several years after being shot in the armed robbery. Since that time, the religion's grip on my mom had continued to tighten. One afternoon when I was 13, my mom walked in on me doing what 13-year-olds sometimes do. I was practicing the age-old art of what the religion labeled "self-abuse." My poor mother! She knew that according to the religion this was sinful and was very worried about what it would lead to. (The cult taught her that it would likely lead to homosexuality, a sin almost as vile as being an apostate). So, she called on the Elders to assist. The Elders are a group of men in the congregation that lead worship, teaching and indoctrination. It's never women, by the way. Women are not allowed to teach in the congregation that would be another rule and another sin if you were keeping track. My mom spoke to one of the Elders and they set up a time to meet with me about my newfound hobby. You can imagine how scared I was walking into that back room at The Kingdom Hall. I remember feeling embarrassed and overwhelmingly ashamed. They read scriptures to me, asked incredibly detailed and intrusive questions, and alluded to the idea that self-abuse leads to homosexuality. And then one of them quoted a scripture regarding fornication. Jesus had said if a man looks at a woman and feels desire for her, he has already committed adultery with her in his heart. The Elder followed up and applied this Bible verse to me by looking me in the eyes and saying, "Michael, usually when a young man does this, he imagines people he knows, maybe even our sisters here in the congregation. You've probably done this yourself. Michael, stop raping our sisters in your heart!"

As if the entire scene wasn't enough, his use of the word rape piled onto my already low self-worth. Helping my young mind accept what a horrible human I had become. I've told that story to a few people and the reaction has been one of horror, which I can appreciate. It's an often-practiced form of spiritual abuse committed by the organization. It shows how pervasive the cult's involvement was in our lives. It also makes me sad about the way my mom had lost her sense of self in placing that parenting situation in someone else's hands. She was searching for answers and a sense of belonging and they handed her easy ones on a platter. She stood loyally by a "God" she had been given by them, while they stripped her of who she was as a person.

That is not to say that I believe they are all bad people, many of the people in the church are like my mom was, genuine and good hearted who are sincere in their beliefs. They are simply misled victims of the mind control used to hold them as captive worker bees. As I grew up, I adopted this belief system and into my mid-20s held onto it like a life preserver in a stormy sea. If alcoholism is a disease that can only be kept at bay by not taking the first drink, then religions like this should be viewed in the same manner.

Three

Enough Coffee Can Fix Anything

After my father was shot robbing a pharmacy we were forced to move again. I'm not sure if it was because, in 1980 even a shithole trailer court didn't want drugs and criminals mucking up the neighborhood, or if we were unable to pay the rent. Whatever the reason, we were out. Semi-nomadic was our way of life. When a problem arose that was too big to face, we moved. There always seemed to be "A better place" that would solve the problem. We lived in nine different places by the time I was 10 years old. At first, there were excuses given. The owner of the house sold it and we needed to move within the week. The landlord didn't like us. Or my personal favorite was the small trailer on the south side of Des Moines where the owner came home from a trip and couldn't figure out why a family with four kids had moved into his home. The righteous indignation by my parents in that scene and the story about being taken advantage of by someone who had said he owned the place was tremendous. I chuckle a little about it today. I always wondered why they didn't explain whose sofa it was that we were sitting on when the guy came home? I'm not saying they were all untruths. I would imagine it mostly came back to not paying the rent or not being an actual tenant at all, but rather simply squatting so we weren't homeless. My parents were doing what they had to do to keep a roof over our heads amidst my father's chaotic, destructive lifestyle of crime and addiction and my mom's clinging onto the cult.

The next place we moved was a small house instead of a trailer. That fact alone was kind of exciting. As a kid I wasn't privy to all of the details of how we found the place and it's difficult to put it exactly in a timeline. I know my father was out of the hospital and recovering and not yet in jail. He was out on pretrial bond. The house was pale yellow located at the end of a dirt road beside a railroad switchyard. The previous people, probably also squatters, had left what seemed to be two feet of junk and garbage filling the house. We all worked to clear it out, first using scoop shovels. Then we carried stuff out by hand. After that, my father used his airless paint sprayer to paint the inside, giving it a fresh clean smell and look. I remember being hopeful when we moved our few belongings into the place. It was summertime so we mostly spent our time outdoors. It was stifling hot that year. We had an uncut yard to play in that concealed garter snakes and toads. And we caught lightening bugs at night. I cringe now at the thought of swinging the snakes by their tail and smacking their heads into the corner of the house. Or pulling the back of the lightening bugs off and smearing them on our fingers so they would glow in the dark.

The train yard was way too tempting for kids and even though it was strictly off limits, we spent a lot of time hopping on and around the slow moving trains looking for what my older brothers called "train whistles." They were metal packing straps for crates that consisted of a thin long strip of metal with holes spaced every inch or so. My brothers would cut a two- or three-inch section of it and bend it in half. Somehow, by doing so they were able to make an ear-piercing whistle from it. I never mastered the technique. Once in a while we would find the small explosive signaling devices used to warn an engineer of something up ahead. They contained a small pack of black powder inside red paper with two soft copper strips that could be bent to hold them on the tracks. When the train rolled over them, they would blow up with a loud bang. When we found them, we replaced the train wheels with bricks dropped from the top step on our porch. It was a fun summer to be a kid. There were lots of dangerous things to play around and almost no supervision. It was easier to put the chaos out of mind with the distractions.

My dad was back to the same lifestyle he had before even though he had an upcoming trial. He was still supporting us, even in a meager way, and his drug addiction through crime. One afternoon I came home to see him in the backyard painting his car with the same airless paint sprayer he used on the inside of the house. Using white latex house paint, he changed the color from dark blue to white in a matter of a couple of hours. My brother told me later the reason he painted it was because he had used it in another armed robbery. The pale-yellow house had a backyard where my mom's wedding ring got lost in the high grass after she took it off and threw it at my dad. I don't know if she ever looked for it, even though they stayed married until he passed away.

Neighborhoods where people live in poverty usually contain two of the same things: dirtballs and drugs. After yet another move, we lived in a different dirt road trailer court that had both. I knew of at least four dealers who sold different substances. Most people there were either selling or using something. Karla and Dave were two of these people. She was in her late 20s with bleach blonde hair and had the figure of someone who used to be attractive. She usually wore a thin button up shirt without a bra and every now and then I would catch a glimpse of her boobs. It was probably the reason I could often be found at their house. Other than boredom or social ineptitude I can't imagine why they wanted to hang around with a kid in the fifth grade. Dave was around the same age as Karla but had lost a lot of his hair on the crown of his head and he kept the sides about shoulder length. For some reason he never wore a shirt, inside or outside. Even then I silently judged him for such a white trash costume.

They were typical. To my knowledge Karla and Dave didn't work and spent most of the day smoking weed. They thought it was funny to get the neighborhood kids high and I was one of their favorites. It became a normal part of my day to knock on Karla and Dave's door. She would give me a couple of dollars to walk to the 7-11 convenience store on the corner and get a few bottles of Pepsi for her. I would help clean the seeds and stems from the cheap weed and then Dave would load the bong and pass it around. Once instead of the normal weed, Dave thought it would be funny to have me smoke something else. I found out later it was PCP. That was a terrifying experience that ended with me trying to get my mom to help me as I erratically explained to her that the demons were speaking through me and my words were not my own. A short time later one of the Elders, Chuck Macheers, was on the phone with me. Strangely in that moment I took a lot of comfort from him. I don't know how long we spoke, but he gradually talked me down and I was a little less frightened. Later, of course, I had to meet with a group of them and endure the scriptural counseling. But if he were still living today, I would tell him thank you for his talking me through that experience.

After my dad went to prison, we lived in a house with one of the "vitamin ladies" from the church. My brothers and I always called a certain group of women "vitamin ladies" A little explanation is in order. In my experience high mind control groups like Jehovah's Witnesses attract the mentally and emotionally ill. People who lack the necessary problem-solving skills to navigate life without easy answers. Since the Jehovah's Witnesses teaching and culture encourages mistrust of the government and in aspects of traditional medicine, some of the people place their belief in vitamin cures and chiropractors who claim to cure anything and everything (including cancer). Naomi was a vitamin lady and a friend of my mom. When I first met her, she was in her late 50s or early 60s and married to a man named Jim. They must have gotten married later in life because I recall going to their wedding reception where they served carrot cake instead of something good. It was probably made without sugar, because in Naomi's mind sugar was poison. One day I was at their house sitting on plastic covered furniture and Naomi confessed to the group that Jim thought she was trying to poison him and was keeping his food and water in a closet under padlock and key. Her adult son was visibly shaken. He muttered the words, "Oh mom not again." *What the fuck did that mean?* I wondered.

Exactly what quality of *again* did this situation hold?

As an adult I sometimes wonder how and why my mom's Spidey sense was so terribly broken.

A few months later, Jim was no longer living there and so my mom, my brothers Mark, Gary and I moved into the two bedrooms in her attic. Naomi would wake us each morning rattling around in the kitchen with the routine of her peculiar "cancer cure" which consisted of vitamins by the handful and then the self-administration of coffee enemas in the bathroom at the bottom of the stairs. Around 6 a.m. you could hear the coffee pot percolating in the kitchen, then shortly after that you could hear Naomi percolating in the bathroom. It was disconcerting to say the least.

After a very short time, Mark moved his bed from the attic bedroom down into the dirt floor basement where he hung old quilts from the floor joists along with a treble light on an extension cord and made a little sectioned off room. He had found (or stolen) an 8-track car stereo and a couple of speakers and had it wired to a car battery so he could listen to Black Sabbath, KISS and anything else that was exactly the opposite of what we were allowed to listen to. Mark was already challenging the constraints of the cult in his own way. I was afraid to go down into that part of the house though because of the rats. In the rest of the house they didn't come out during the day, only at night. But in that basement, it was common to see one scurry across the floor just a few feet from you. At night they became more emboldened. One night I remember feeling something on top of my blanket, so I flipped my blanket and a big rat sailed through the air and landed in the middle of the room where it scurried off.

As time progressed the rats got worse. One night, while my mom was reading a book to Gary and me, we heard something scratching behind the dresser. My feet instinctually pulled up to my chest and I tightened the blanket around myself. Gary, on the other hand, leapt from the bed, grabbed a broom and jabbed it into the crack between the dresser and the wall poking the fat little bastard until it came running across the floor with my brother in hot pursuit. It had made it to the top of the steps by the time he was able to line up his shot and take a swing. Using the handle of the broom with the precision of an NHL player he sent it sailing through the air over the steps toward the opposite wall where it hit with a thud. It fell to the lower landing where it promptly ran into the bathroom and down a hole we discovered in the wall behind the toilet. Gary was always like that. I was the timid one and he took action. After that incident, via urging from my mom, Naomi decided something should probably be done about the rat infestation. In that terrifying basement near Marks "bedroom" beside the stairs there was a small crawl space. We were told this was the main nest area of the rats and we were under extremely strict orders from Naomi never to go near it. When Naomi poisoned the rats, the entire house began to smell like something dead and rotting and it was then that she had the crawl space walled over with cinder block, leaving a child to wonder exactly what horrors were back there. I guess the rats should have invested in a padlock for their food and water, or perhaps Jim should have invested in a better one.

Four

The Saddest Words Ever Spoken

My father was sent to the Iowa State Penitentiary in Fort Madison, Iowa, where he remained for a number of years. It looked exactly the way you imagine when you picture a prison in your mind: ancient high grey granite walls with a guard tower atop each corner giving off the look of a medieval fortress. It was built in 1839, seven years before Iowa became a state. As a child visiting this place, it felt ominous and foreboding. Along with the small amount of joy from getting to see my father, I would also feel a sense of dread overtake me.

Because Fort Madison was about 180 miles from where we lived, we didn't get to make the trip terribly often. By this time, mom was without a car so when we were able to go, we carpooled with one of the other families visiting a relative. There seemed to be some type of system from within the prison that put families in contact with one another. It was something like a family ride share organized by the prisoners. By doing this, the families could share the expense of the trip. Since we had almost no money the trips were only occasional.

Sherry, a frumpy middle-aged white woman who never smiled, was the person who drove the most often. Her husband was serving a life sentence. She had married him after he was incarcerated. My judgment was that she had a small brain. I don't know why I drew that conclusion. She was what I considered to be joyless, kind of pear shaped with short brown hair and thin lips that caused me to mistrust her. She continually chomped on strong smelling gum. I recall the pungent smell inside the AMC station wagon being a mix of mint and bad breath.

During some of the trips, her stepson Tyrone would also be along for the ride. I didn't know Tyrone other than the six-hour round trip rides from Des Moines to Fort Madison. On one early ride I asked him, "Why are you with her? Where's your mom, why isn't she taking you?" His clipped answer painted the picture too well, "My daddy killed my mamma." Today his use of the word "mamma" is one of the saddest words I've ever heard. Yet at the time that didn't seem odd. If he had told me his mom was out of town because she had a work appointment it would have been more out of place.

I wish I could say I felt compassion for Tyrone, but I didn't. On those trips my younger self hated him. Just looking at him made me mad. Tyrone was a year or two older than me, a chunky kid with ashy skin and thick arms. He always wore a frown. If he wasn't angry I think he would have cried a lot more. Today when I think of him I think of sadness. On most occasions when our words became too tiresome, we would end up in a fist fight in the back of the station wagon. My ego would like to tell you I won those fights, but the truth is I seldom did. By the time the adults got the car pulled over he would have me pinned somehow, punching me in the face or in the ribs. Tyrone was a tough kid. I won some, but mostly he did. I guess he had more to be angry about. Today when I think of him I think of the sadness and anger we both had. I think about this poor kid whose father had murdered his mother. He was living in foster care and bouncing to a strange woman's home to take a trip to see his dad and then facing off with another angry kid instead of someone who should have been his friend. I hope Tyrone has found some peace since then.

On those trips we would always be picked up early, before sunrise, on Saturday in order to be waiting at the prison the moment visiting hours began. After walking through the front doors, you'd go past a few offices into a small waiting room, where my mom would fill out paperwork and hand it back to the apathetic guards through a set of bars. Then after waiting for what felt like an eternity, our name would be called. The waiting was excruciating. The three or four guards we could see were sectioned off from us by bars in the pre-visit search area. And just beyond them was another wall of bars where the general prison population was housed.

We would often stand at that first wall of bars and watch for a glimpse of our dad. It was there that he would walk past shortly before we would be called to enter the visiting room.

The pre-visit search area had a table with a tray where anything in your pockets was deposited. Hot wheels cars and little green army men felt out of place in that scene. Then there was a metal detector to walk through. After walking through the metal detector, one of the guards would pat everyone down head-to-toe. Then, another guard would use a key from the big ring of keys he held to open a barred door into a stairwell. We would file into the stairwell and hear the door clang shut behind us. It was this same stairwell where we were locked in for more than two hours in 1981 when a riot broke out in the prison. The riot lasted 11 hours, multiple prison employees were beaten and at least one prisoner was murdered.

Past the stairwell we walked to the top of a flight of steps where we waited a minute or two until the electric motor on the solid metal door would loudly run and roll it to one side. After walking through that door, it would close behind us and directly in front stood a window with a two-way mirror through which you couldn't see. On either side was a different automatic metal door. One door led to an unventilated room filled with headache causing clouds of cigarette smoke and the other led to my father.

The door to the left would grind open and he would be standing there smiling, dressed in his light blue shirt with the number 200565 printed just above where a pocket should have been. I would run to him wrapping my arms around him and for the briefest of moments everything was alright.

We sat in hard chairs around a low table all competing to be heard. I would hang on every one of his words. There were words about a picture he was painting or one detailing how many miles he had run on the track in the yard. Out of those words I was able to create a reality that removed all culpability from my dad, one where he didn't make the choice to be separated from us. The reality I imagined was one where he didn't leave us but was taken against his will. In some respects, I suppose that was true, in others he certainly made choices that placed him behind bars. As a child, I think it was better though to believe he genuinely WANTED to be with us but was forced not to be. Maybe by thinking that, it made a difference between feeling abandoned and just feeling scared and alone. There is a feeling of loss that goes with purposeful abandonment that I did not have to suffer by holding this belief. Beliefs are like that; we can easily begin to believe things that fill up some void in us whether they are true or not. This belief that it wasn't my father's fault that he was incarcerated and away from us was cemented early on when visiting him by the ever-present voice that would come over the speaker in the room. We would hear, "Too much contact between the child and the inmate, separate." Or if he and my mom had stolen a kiss or hugged too long it would say, "There isn't enough distance between the female and the inmate." And so, if I were climbing into his lap or hugging him, or just merely standing too close, I was forced to move away. Not by him but by someone else. These things provided me with the evidence I needed to hold on to my belief that this wasn't his fault, it was someone else's.

On another memorable trip my brother Mark and I were looking through the bars across the guarded pre-visit search section into the general population area watching the inmates file past. We were watching for a glimpse of our dad. The men were walking single-file parallel to the bars when we saw one prisoner's arm draw back at the elbow and jab something sharp a number of times into the man in front of him. The man in front jerked a little and fell to the floor where he stayed motionless. What I remember next is a flurry of people running and shouting. Through the bars, the guards were yelling at one another, the inmates becoming a roar of unintelligible voices and my mom grabbing me by the arm and pulling me away where I couldn't see it anymore.

All visits were canceled that day and I remained confused by what I saw. During the excited but frightened conversation on the way home, I was quiet. I know now that I saw a stranger being murdered that day.

The effect that incarceration of a parent has on the emotional growth and wellbeing of a child is something I am passionate about. Prisons have changed since I had to visit my father in that environment. In some ways for the better. Most old prisons have been replaced with newer facilities, in part to keep prisoners safer from the violence they live with every day. But, also, to house more prisoners because the incarceration rate has increased dramatically. What does it say about us when we lock people away for nonviolent offenses and at the same time, turn it into an industry of profit by outsourcing incarceration of our citizens to large corporations? The people who are jailed for nonviolent drug offenses would be better served by treating it as a medical problem rather than a legal one. Also, the way children and families of inmates are viewed and treated has not changed. The children and families of people who are incarcerated are largely viewed and treated with the same amount of disdain the prisoners are. While neither the prisoner nor the family need be disrespected or mistreated, when we treat children of inmates without respect, compassion, kindness, and dignity as a fellow human, we are perpetuating the problem of drug abuse, addiction and crime. The idea that children of inmates are in many ways our best route to decreasing future crime seems to be lost. Instead of seeing small kindnesses and education as the mechanism to keep that kid from being the next generation populating the prison. Many working in the penal system either actively show they dislike these kids, or at the very least treat them with apathy. I don't, however, want to group everyone together; some are caring compassionate people. But as a whole, the system is bent toward not caring what happens to the child of an offender. I don't know what the answer is, but I do have questions we can ask to figure it out.

- *How can we teach a kid he or she has a future bigger than prison when his or her identity is wrapped up with someone who has committed crime and is incarcerated?*
- *How can we shore up the emotional welfare of the child of an offender and give him or her a sense of value?*
- *How can we change our spending to better serve this group, knowing that in the bigger picture not only is it the right thing to do but it also costs less to help a child than to incarcerate an adult?*
- *How can we change the mindset of the children themselves to see prison employees and police officers as something better than an opponent?*
- *How can we give these children the opportunity to understand why their parent has been incarcerated yet at the same time not cause further damage to the bond between parent and child?*
- *And how can we help prison employees and police to see and care about their part in all of this?*

Five

The (Un)Breakable Bond of Brotherhood

Through all the chaos and always with me was my brother and absolute best friend Gary. Although only two years older, he seemed like an adult to me. Perhaps that's how we invariably view big brothers. My mom described that when we were small, he would help me dress, straighten my collar, make sure my shirt was tucked in and so forth. His nature was always that of a caretaker, and not just with me, but with others as well. I certainly filled the role of a baby brother for him. Even into my adult years I constantly gave him someone who needed looking after. If I needed money or work, he was there. If my car broke down, he was there. If I needed advice when my father let us down, he seemed to fill in. The fact that he was able to do that is strange to me because as small kids Gary was the one who was closer to my father. I would have thought it affected him more than me when our father went away. I often saw him as my dad's favorite, but it never bothered me in a way that made me feel jealous. Gary was the one who sat in my father's lap at breakfast and sipped little drinks of his coffee with him. He was the first one my dad would pick up and greet with a hug when he got home. Because of this it seemed odd that I ended up being the one following in my father's footsteps down a road of criminal behavior and addiction. For the most part, Gary was the responsible one, not that he didn't have his incidents, as any kid would. Around the same time I was getting high most days with the neighbors Karla and Dave, Gary who was in the seventh grade had also been going through a rough time emotionally and had been refusing to go to school. So, after missing much of the seventh grade, he was hospitalized in an adolescent behavioral unit to help figure out what was wrong. I don't know what the exact diagnosis was, but if I were to look it up, I imagine it was probably anxiety and depression. Living in a dysfunctional family dynamic with a criminal father while also trying to live up to our mother's expectation of our life in the religion would likely do that to most anyone. When he came home from the hospital, he told lots of stories about his time there. He mentioned his doctor on more than one occasion. He described him as a man who genuinely seemed caring. I suppose Gary was searching for a father figure in the absence of ours. His school attendance and performance improved after that, but like me, he was still a delinquent.

One afternoon while we were out playing, Gary looked me in the eyes and said, "I'm gonna steal that truck," pointing to a truck across the dirt road. It was a rusty behemoth that wasn't exactly the size of a pickup, and not as big as a semi either, but somewhere in between. It was used to move the mobile homes into and out of the trailer court. It would show up from time to time when they moved something and then stay parked in front of our trailer for a while. It had been there for a couple of days when the idea of taking it began to fester in his mind. "You shouldn't do that Gary, it's Ernie's," I said. Ernie was the bald hawk-faced guy who owned the trailer court and most of the trailers in it. "I'm just gonna take it and drive it around. It's not like I won't bring it back. He won't even know it's gone." I decided he wasn't serious or even if he was, he probably didn't know how to steal a car anyway.

But Gary wasn't a person who just talked about doing things he took action. Sure enough, he stole the truck and drove it around all day until it ran out of gas and then left it in the middle of a street somewhere and walked home. When the police found it a few days later and came to the trailer court asking folks what they knew, someone recalled seeing him messing with it and sent them in our direction. It's an odd coincidence that Gary was just a bit older than my dad had been when he was first sent to the boys' home in Eldora Iowa for stealing cars. Gary didn't face that penalty though, and perhaps his life took a different path because of the leniency he was shown. He was charged with joy riding, had to pay a fine and received some community service. He didn't get into much trouble at home over it; I think my mom was glad that it wasn't grand theft. Or maybe she had become so accustomed to having the police knocking on our door due to our dad, that she didn't react as expected. That or she was simply worn out from the years of abnormal control placed on her by the church alongside the insecurity of our family.

Even though he had some troubles of his own, when I would do something that he thought was past the line Gary would let me know. It was his disapproval more than anyone else that felt the worst. One time when he caught me with a janky pot-pipe I had fashioned out of a toilet paper roll and tin foil, he ripped it from my hands, tore it apart, and gave me a beating. Getting beat up by an older brother is just a rite of passage and it happened often. I remember this one, though; because in catching me I could tell it hurt him in some way I didn't understand. Older brothers are a funny thing. Gary tried extremely hard to fill a role that he never should have had to fill, yet for me being a younger brother the idea that he would do anything different never crossed my mind.

Amidst the crazy backdrop of visiting my father in prison and continuously being force-fed the mind controlling dogma of our religion, we still found a place for happiness and fun. When I think about good times in my childhood, summers with Gary are the most memorable. I'd be sitting in anticipation waiting for the last bell on the last day of school before summer vacation would begin. The final hours seemed endless. I remember feeling restless at my desk like a jittery racehorse in the starting gates. I was practically shaking with excitement. Then the final bell would ring and everyone would run out of the classroom with the teacher saying, "walk," to deaf ears. My end of school year papers that were supposed to go home would inevitably go flying over my shoulder into the hallway. Litter was strewn to the point where it looked like a movie theatre after the show. Papers pulled out of lockers piled high along the walls, pouring out and across the tile hallway where a few sheets would meet in the middle. The rolling trashcans being used by so few sat almost empty. If only one kid had made a mess like that surely something would have been done about it. But since it was almost everyone the teachers had long since given up on that final day. Leaving the mess for the custodian beginning his summer routine was an ugly reminder of the rottenness of youth. Then as I made my way out the doors of the school, I would find Gary waiting for me, to watch over me as we walked home.

We were never without fun or the ability to get into trouble in the summertime. We'd leave home as soon as we awoke in the morning and return as the sun was sinking off in the west. Riding our bikes, playing in creeks, going to the pool, playing basketball, those were the times I almost felt like a normal kid from a normal family. Gary and I were always together then. If one of us got in trouble, we both did. If someone wanted to fight, they had to fight both of us. If one of us figured out how to scrounge some spare change to buy a pop or ice cream, we shared it. Back then, the bond felt unbreakable. I didn't realize though how subversive my mother's religion could be.

Six

A Hatchet, a Puppet, and the Woolco Store

After my father was sent to prison, much of the influence that conflicted with the religion came from my two oldest brothers, Paul and Mark. They often rebelled against the hundreds of rules placed on us, both in their words and their actions. This influence left when they left home. Paul left when he was 15 years old, and Mark followed just a year or two later. That left Gary and I without anyone that we were close to and trusted to imprint upon us ideas or actions except the people we were surrounded by in the church. With this as my only touchstone, one based in fear of Armageddon, persecution by the government, Satan, the demons and fear of losing my friends and family, little by little I began to adopt the beliefs of my mom's religion. This resulted in easing some of my mom's worries about raising juvenile delinquents.

I was growing into an awkward, tall, skinny kid wearing big goofy glasses who was painfully introverted and quiet. I had grown very quickly over the last couple of years and was often embarrassed by the high-water pants I always seemed to be wearing. This, along with very little socialization outside of the Witnesses, resulted in a painful shyness rooted in extremely low self-esteem.

Describing this time between childhood and when I finally escaped the cult is a bit like trying to describe the color grey. There are only so many words to use before it becomes very repetitive. Mind control feels like that. There is a great deal of repetition, a constant pressure of sameness day in and day out, week in and week out, year in and year out. There isn't any change and very little excitement. It makes difficult subject matter to keep you, the reader, engaged. So if my story seems to pass many years without explanation this is why. It's with this pressure of repetitious messaging and lack of excitement that people become trapped within the confining atmosphere of high mind control groups. It's a hypnosis of sorts, where the free-thinking mind goes to sleep continuously hearing the same repetitive instruction of Armageddon nearing. The message tells you you're one of God's *chosen* people, and yet not worthy at the same time. That conflicted idea of being *chosen but not worthy* was successful in keeping me within the Jehovah's Witness organization for many years. It instilled in me the belief that being worthy comes from deeds that should be close to perfection instead of the belief I have today that each of us has a place in this Universe simply because we exist. This rightful place in the Universe has nothing to do with something we must earn.

As the years dragged on, nothing out of the ordinary, at least to us, happened. I'd wake up, go to school, come home, go to the Kingdom Hall, read the bible, read the books printed by the Watchtower, and stay asleep. I took my solace in reading other books not written by The Watchtower. I could spend hours in a library getting lost, and I especially loved reading about any sort of adventure. Books like *Call of the Wild*, *20,000 Leagues Under the Sea*, *Tom Sawyer*, and *Treasure Island* became my escape and the characters my friends. *Huckleberry Finn* was my favorite. I read it dozens of times. I could get lost in the story of Huck finding a log raft on the river and floating away on it. That was exactly what I wanted to do. I thought anywhere but here would be better. Yet I hadn't developed any vision beyond the confines of my reality within the constricted nature of the cult. So I mostly existed in that space in my head of "later" or "somewhere else." It was a space of imagination and hope that was never completely taken from me even during my years of belief in the teachings of the church.

It was in this same timeframe that the Woolco store a few blocks from our dingy trailer court was preparing to close down. Woolco was a discount Department Store that had racks and racks full of everything under the sun. The chain was owned by HG Woolworth and Company and went out of business in the U.S. in 1982. Having been taught a mindset of scarcity, both because we lived in poverty and due to the teaching that we should spend our time proselytizing not bettering our situation but being content with just the necessities of life, I would walk through the store in wonder looking up at the high shelves with big eyes thinking almost everything was something I would never be able to afford. One summer my mom told us she was going to have $12 left in her budget and she wanted to spend it on Gary and me. On her next payday in two weeks, we could each buy something from the store before it closed. She was giving us $6 each! That seemed very extravagant in my small world. After she told us about it, I would go there every day walking through the front doors into the brightly lit store and down through the aisles, looking for something I might like to purchase with this upcoming wealth. There were racks and racks of clothes, and a shelf that held the cheap blue tennis shoes that we usually received at the start of a new school year. I remember them vividly because when they were soaked through from walking through the snow the color would bleed and turn our feet blue. It was probably some sort of cheap 1970s-era dye that is outlawed now due to causing toenails to fall out, cancer of the toes, and infertility.

I walked down an aisle of board games and considered a few. Then I wandered into the electronics section and stood and watched the TVs on display for a little while. I meandered past the picked over plastic toys, taking my time to pick up and inspect each of them. So far, I couldn't imagine parting with the $6 for anything I had seen, or at the very least anything I had seen that I could afford. I felt discouraged. I then aimlessly wandered into the hardware section and there on the shelf they hung: a rack full of small axes. I picked one up and swung it like I was chopping down an imaginary tree. The little axe had a pine handle and a blackened steel head. It felt like freedom when I held it. I stood looking at it, holding it up to the light, inspecting each detail, and turning it over in my hand. With the axe in my hand I lived in my imaginary world where I built a log raft that I would float away on. It must have looked strange, or even scary, for people to see a skinny, goofy-looking kid swinging a hatchet back and forth in a department store. If they could have seen the adventures I was having in my mind, though, they would have understood. I returned every day to look at the little axes. It was a way to live out my fantasy for a little while until reality returned.

You might be confused as to how we lived in what appears to be several distinct realities that seemed to be separate from one another. How did living in an imaginary world in my own head space, while smoking pot, stealing, and skipping school live in concert with going to church for hours, bible study every night and knocking on doors to convert non-believers? Living dual realities is very common for JW young people and adults. The church would call it "living a double life." It's an abhorrent idea to them. The pressure of growing up and living in their world caused me to hide anything that wouldn't fit their narrow view of what is acceptable. As time passed, the habit of hiding anything that would stand out as wrong became ingrained in me. Even small things. Small things would later turn to larger more serious things. As a kid if I strayed even in a ridiculously small way, like eating a cupcake during a classroom birthday party, I knew not to talk about it at home. The environment was such that I wouldn't even share that with other JW kids who were my friends. To do so would risk having them speak to the Elders and being called in for scriptural counseling. It is taught that to know of someone else's *'wrongdoing'* and not speak up is the same as committing the sin yourself. This culture of spying on one another became completely ingrained in the group of friends I grew up with. With this influence, a great deal of dishonesty became part of who I was and how I navigated the world, out of necessity. It began as more of a survival skill than anything else. Yet in time it became a very flawed character trait in many ways. My dishonesty as an addict and alcoholic led to hurting the people I loved the most.

The days during those two weeks seemed to just creep past. Each day felt longer than the last. When I returned to look over my soon-to-be had gift each day, the supply was fewer and fewer. The day before my mother's payday there was just one left. I carried it to the checkout and asked hopefully, "This is the last of these and I would like to buy it tomorrow, could you keep it here for me so someone else doesn't buy it?" Without even looking at me, he said that they couldn't do that. I hung my head and walked it back to the rack. I went home nervous and anxious that it would be gone the next afternoon but excited and hopeful. I wonder if this is what the time leading up to Christmas Eve felt like to other kids.

As I lay in bed that night, Huck and Jim were paddling their canoe from Jackson's Island toward a house that the flooded Mississippi had washed down the river. I drifted off to sleep aboard my own little raft, already a part of their story.

The next day dawned with excitement for both Gary and me. We watched the bus stop all day for our mom to return from work. When the bus finally brought her home, she was met with two excited and unruly boys jabbering away at her. As the three of us walked the few blocks to the department store, I felt happy. The sun was shining, and the air was warm. My mother seemed happy that day. I suppose not having many opportunities to spend money on her children, this special treat of a $6 gift for us made her feel cheerful and upbeat. "Have you decided what it is you want?" she asked us. Words tumbled out of me as I excitedly described to her the little axe and all the things I could do with it. She looked at me, not with the tired look that she usually wore, but instead with a content smile on her face.

When we walked into the Woolco store, I noticed the shelves had taken on an abandoned look. They were picked over and cleared out as they sold off all their inventory before closing their doors for the last time. I ran off toward the section where my axe was, and Gary went in a different direction. I don't recall what it was my mom bought for him that day, probably a few tools or wrenches. He was often tinkering on old things and building bicycles out of old parts that were lying around our yard. When I rounded the corner and went down the half-bare aisle, my heart sank. The rack where the object of my imaginary escape from reality had been hanging just the day before sat empty. The disappointment felt overwhelming. I can understand now that the axe became just a symbol I fixated on, and many of the choked back feelings from my life came rushing up making it feel much larger than it was. But even with that knowledge it remains a raw moment firmly rooted in me.

As I walked back toward the front of the store, I thought about my mom's smile and the happiness she had in giving me this gift. I walked past a shopping cart and noticed it was full of a mishmash of different items picked up by an employee during the melee of the going out of business sale. I stopped and began rummaging through the items. There was a pair of pliers, a lime green girl's sweater, a few fly swatters, and then I found a toy puppet: Rowlf from *The Muppet Show*. He was the brown dog that played the piano. I looked it over and put my hand inside of it to move his wide mouth open and closed. I listlessly carried it with me as I returned to find my mom. I held it up and then handed it to her. She took the animated brown puppet from my outstretched arm and held it toward me opening his mouth with her hand and pretended to bite my nose with it. I smirked as she did. "Why did you change your mind?" she asked. "I like this more," I said. And her smile remained.

Seven

Everyone Should Own a Cadillac

Friendships as a Witness kid develop in a similar way as they do for everyone else. One exception that I speculate about today is the depth those friendships take on due to the belief in the impending doom for the rest of the world. The group takes on a feeling of family. We shared a common bond of being a small group of chosen would-be survivors surrounded by everyone else who was just too ignorant or evil to see things the same way. Now I see the bond as one where people share a common trauma. The few friends I have today from childhood, who have also given up the religion, share a history and memories that are difficult to explain to others. Even in writing many chapters about the effects—mentally, emotionally and physically—of growing up in the group, I hesitate to think I have adequately described the true impact of it. Because of this history, these friendships still feel like family. Chad is a friend who I share that brotherly bond with.

During the summer I was 16, two things happened: Chad and I decided to take a road trip together, and I met a girl I was crazy about. We met at a wedding in another small town in Iowa and I was smitten with her immediately. Her name was Connie. We began corresponding and calling each other whenever we could. Rarely seeing one another in person though. Even calling one another and writing letters was behind the backs of our parents because, until marriage is an option, Witnesses are not allowed to date. We would write letters to one another by mailing them to a mutual friend who would pass them along to the other person. Phone calls were difficult since this was before cell phones and long-distance rates were insanely high. I found a short-term solution to this when I saw an advertisement in a magazine for a Sprint long distance calling card. I made the call and a short time later a shiny silver card showed up in the mail with my name on it. I only had to dial a few extra numbers from the card and the long-distance charges never showed up on the phone bill at home. It was like magic. By giving the magic numbers from the card to Connie, she could do the same. This ended abruptly when my mom received a call from Sprint one day asking when the $700 phone bill would be paid. I wasn't very good at thinking ahead back then.

The rush of first love is immense for anyone. Adding to this for myself, and I believe for her as well, was the underlying feeling of being trapped by our religion. Although I didn't recognize it at the time, being in love felt like the escape. Something overwhelmingly positive amidst the gloom and doom. Within a noticeably short period of time, we began talking about our future life together. We talked about marriage and becoming "Pioneers," devoting our full-time effort to proselytizing and attempting to convert others.

That summer, Chad's dad Phil, a kind and generous man who always wore a smile, let us use his Cadillac for our trip, as neither of us had a car that was reliable enough. My 1971 Volkswagen Beatle wouldn't get across town without breaking down, let alone take a 1500-mile road trip out of state. The Cadillac Deville was a beautiful new car with lush, comfortable leather seats. And since gas was under a buck a gallon back then even the big V-8 engine was a bonus. We scraped together what we could from part-time jobs, mine at Godfather's Pizza and Chad's at McDonalds, threw a few clothes into bags and set off for the mountains of Colorado. Our plan was to sleep in the car with a return date of "when our money ran out." Up to this point I had barely been outside of Iowa, except to travel to Witness conventions in Nebraska. Four long days each summer we'd sit in hard chairs listening to the ever-repetitive message of how terrible things were in the world (crime violence wars and famine), which was evidence we were living in the last days and Armageddon was almost upon us.

The afternoon we left, I took the first shift driving and my inexperience with travel was apparent from the start. With "Going to California" by Led Zeppelin playing, at the edge of

Des Moines where Interstates 35 and 80 cross, I piloted the big comfortable Cadillac south out of Des Moines headed for Kansas City instead of west toward Colorado. One hundred miles or so into the trip Chad noticed we were off track and by consulting an old road atlas we found an alternate route west through Kansas. Kansas is a wide and flat place when traveling by interstate. So as Chad fell asleep in the backseat, my foot became heavier on the accelerator and the large car ate up the miles. Even driving nearly 100 miles per hour it was like sitting on a big comfy couch as the wheat field scenery whipped past the side windows. Everyone should own a Cadillac at some point in their life and drive it recklessly fast across the state of Kansas. Sometime after dark we pulled off to sleep through the night after I had fallen asleep behind the wheel and narrowly missed a stalled car on the shoulder, the rumble strips waking me at the last minute.

The next day we reached our first destination: Georgetown, Colorado, a small town up the mountain from Denver where a Witness friend a few years older than us had moved with his wife. (A few years later, Chad moved to this same town and I moved just down the mountain in the foothills of Golden). On this trip, spending time here with other Witnesses was a reminder of the controlled existence I had left just the day before. The conversation fell into the all too familiar questions about our plans for the future in the church and also how close the end of this evil world must be. Would we be volunteering at "Bethel" after High School (the world headquarters of the Watchtower)? Would we become Regular

Pioneers? (A volunteer position that required 90 hours each month to be spent in the door-to-door ministry work) I immediately wanted to move on. It felt like the freedom I was feeling was pulled away. It was like the abrupt stop when a surprised dog gets to the end of a chain.

Leaving Georgetown, we spent the day white water rafting on the Colorado River and spent the evening sunburned and drinking beers we weren't supposed to have laughing at nothing with newfound friends. We were regular teenagers. The following days we bounced around with no real destination, just rambling down mountain roads listening to Led Zeppelin, and Edie Brickell, taking in the scenery, hiking up trails, watching waterfalls, sleeping in the car, eating bologna and bread, and staring at the mountains. Time flew past doing nothing and everything.

One morning I woke to windows that had a foggy dew on the inside from our breath through the night. Chad was asleep in the front seat. I sleepily climbed out of the back walking on tender feet across the gravel to the back of the car to pee. As sleep slowly left my eyes I began to take in the scenery of the place. The mountain valley was filled with aspen trees, it had a chill of the sort very distinct to valleys where the cool air of the mountain settles at night. The birds were singing, the rippling of water from a river could be heard close by and I almost tasted the smell of the mist in the air. I had an imprinting moment where a sense of stillness entered my mind and inner peace quieted all of the noise in my head. With it an amazing feeling of being free swept through me in a way that can only be felt by someone who has long been held captive. I am sure I stood there that morning at the crossroads of the path my life would take for many years. The memory of that moment of stillness never left me though.

Returning home, the feeling of freedom faded but never quite left. Connie and I continued corresponding. Her family was very entrenched in the faith and extremely well-respected. Her father was an Elder, presiding over a small congregation, and her older sister and brother-in-law worked full-time and lived at the Watchtower headquarters in New York. In the Witness culture Connie and I came from different worlds. I set out to make myself a respectable *"brother"* in the congregation, taking the faith more and more seriously and trying to grow *"spiritually"* enough to fit in, to be good enough. That continuous thought process and attempt to be "good enough" was as much a part of me as the color of my hair. I think this is something many people can identify with. Personally, because of my lack of autonomy and no clear vision of who I wanted to be, apart from the organization's narrow view of what is acceptable, I drifted into the belief that I always needed to be doing something in order to be ok. My thoughts continually returned to how I was not living up to God's perfect standard of living. To have a place in this Universe, I had learned that I needed to earn it in some way. The concept of grace was altogether unknown and foreign. And so, inner peace and serenity were also quite absent.

Shortly before I turned 19, Connie and I were married. Even within our restricted minds, severely limited by our beliefs, those first years were happy because we were very much in love. We lived simply, without much money but somewhat content with the idea we were serving God. A life purpose was fed to us, as we worked through the days knocking on people's doors trying to convert them to a life of salvation rather than destruction at Armageddon.

Looking back, I appreciate the tremendous real-life sales training I received by knocking on all of those doors. Later that sales training served me well in a successful career. I often make the joke, if you can sell The Watchtower's version of God you can sell ABSOLUTELY anything. I also gained experience as a public speaker traveling to surrounding congregations to deliver the Sunday sermons to similarly blind followers. There living in a modest house in a small Iowa town devoting ourselves to The Watchtower's work. Several years passed but it wouldn't be long before the emotionally damaging environment would take its toll on both Connie and me.

Eight

When Life Breaks Down

I woke up in the middle of the night with a start. *What did I hear?* It sounded like it was coming from the back of the house. It was either the door or a window opening. My breath became shallow and quick as my heart raced, listening through the quiet to hear it again. Someone was in the house. *Why were they here?* They were here to hurt us. I was sure of that. I quietly placed my hand on my wife's arm. I whispered, "I think there's someone in the house. Stay quiet and stay here." Her eyes were wide with fear.

I reached beside the bed and put my hand on the baseball bat that I kept within easy reach against the wall. I quietly got up and slipped through the door out of the bedroom holding it in both hands near my shoulder ready to swing. I stopped just through the door and listened. Still no sound. Perhaps the intruder had heard me moving. I waited for my eyes to adjust to the dim light, watching for any sign of movement. I finally willed myself to move again and crept toward the back of the house. I moved into the hallway bathroom, but it seemed to be empty. As I approached the shower curtain, I felt a cold chill down my spine. I slid the curtain back. Nobody. Once I was sure the bathroom was safe, I advanced through the kitchen. The noise had come from this direction I was sure of it. Though I had checked all the locks several times before going to bed I checked the handle of the back door again. It was still locked. The window to the left of it remained closed. That left only one additional room to check. I wiped one clammy hand and then the other on my shorts regripping the bat. I looked at the closed door that led into the last bedroom. *Had I closed this door earlier? Why couldn't I remember?* I slowly turned the doorknob and gently pushed. As the door opened, I took a step back readying myself for the attacker … but nothing. I reached in and quickly flipped the light switch. There was nobody there.

I retraced my steps through the house turning on all the lights as I went, my heart continuing to race. I returned for a moment to tell my wife that, once again, there was no danger. After going through my increasingly more frequent routine I knew it was another false alarm. I poured a glass of bourbon to calm my nerves and sat down in a chair. I knew it would be hours until daybreak when the fear, anxiety and adrenalin would subside, and I could fall back to sleep.

It had been several years since Connie and I were married. The pressure of growing up and living under the fear of the

Jehovah's Witnesses, coupled with being left without tools to deal with the experience of my father's criminal life and his battle with addiction, had slowly taken its toll. About six years earlier, we were totally entrenched in a life of servitude under the control of the organization, yet we still harbored a sense of adventure and wanting more than the limited way of life we were living. Staying within the boundaries built in our minds, we crafted a plan to first move to Des Moines and serve in a Spanish language congregation, and then later we would move to Central or South America to work and live our lives as missionaries for The Watchtower. Thankfully, the missionary part never happened. In fact, I am happy to report that in all my years as a Witness I didn't ever successfully convert a single person!

Looking back, I believe a wonderful thing came out of moving back to Des Moines and transferring to the Spanish congregation. Since I did not speak Spanish, it gave my mind an ever so slight respite from the continuous dogma and propaganda of the Watchtower. Instead of actively participating in my own brainwashing every week at the church services, I struggled to understand what was being said and concentrated instead on learning a new language while I attended services in this new foreign language congregation. Also, before the move, I had advanced quickly within the Witness hierarchy and was told I would very soon be an Elder. That fed my ego tremendously. I became a self-righteous jerk in so many ways, actively taking part in the breaking down of other people's autonomy and ability to make their own decisions, making others feel shame and fear.

I'll give an example; one I am not proud of today. It had become known that a woman in our congregation was dating someone who was not a Jehovah's Witness. So, in preparing my sermon for the upcoming church service, I researched all the Watchtower literature I could find about "marrying only in the lord" and created a scathing sermon on the subject. When I delivered the sermon, I looked directly at her and no one else, piously making her feel small and not good enough. I showed no compassion to this poor woman. Sitting with her friends and family, I singled her out and bullied her from the podium. I preached that falling in love with a non-believer was the same as having no love for God and alluded to the idea that dating a non-believer would most certainly result in immorality and disfellowshipping. I did this to a lovely woman who was innocent and doing nothing wrong, she was simply dating someone she wanted to date and deciding for herself as she should have! She was an innocent soul who wanted what everyone wants: to just be happy. Today I feel so sorry for what I put her through, for my lack of compassion and for the embarrassment and shame she must have felt because I was a sanctimonious dick!

My ego was also fed heartily by my natural ability to speak in front of a group and keep them entertained, which ended because I could no longer adequately communicate from the stage due to the language barrier in the Spanish congregation. It's a strange dynamic that is developed in high mind control groups. First the person's ability and willingness to choose for themselves is taken away and self-esteem is largely broken down, and then the ego is fed when the person does things that agree with what the group thinks. Without the continuous stroking of my ego in this way, and with the slight distance from the propaganda, my resolve shifted some. My belief remained fixed on the nearness of Armageddon and in The Watchtower's role as the only voice of God, but my motivation and resolve in my actions and plans changed. I know now that Connie's resolve was also shifting, though we never spoke about it. Because to speak about it, even to a spouse, one risked sounding apostate to the other. To be an apostate or a traitor who questions the Watchtower (considered God's chosen mouthpiece) in any way is believed unforgivable even by God himself.

Connie and I had different symptoms from the same pressure and fear. Because of the trauma, she developed anorexia, bulimia, and depression. I battled depression and anxiety. When the anxiety became severe, I began to show many symptoms of PTSD and finally turned to alcoholism and addiction. Yet we were both left with the belief that at the core was a spiritual problem, something that was lacking in our devotion to God and his plan. Something that more bible study and more activity in the church should alleviate. It's little wonder that I later wrote off the idea of God altogether.

We began distancing ourselves from the Witnesses. Slowly at first and not completely on purpose. While Connie suffered from anorexia, which left her hospitalized twice, the

Elders in the congregation removed me from my position as a Ministerial Servant, (this is the precursor to becoming an Elder). They also stripped us both of our title as Pioneers or full-time door-to-door ministers. The entire foundation of self-worth had been built on my belief in the cult, my actions for the church and my ego in my position. With the position gone, my ego tumbled, and my anxiety and depression worsened. I found no inner peace and spiraled downward emotionally. As Connie found professional help, I became more and more anxious and depressed. What I discovered was that I could use alcohol to bring relief. I also found myself adrift without purpose. Until now, we had the shared purpose of our life as Witnesses and our plans around that. Now all of that seemed to be slipping away. The social structure of the group was gradually replaced with loneliness and an inability to fit into a different world because I carried with me all of the beliefs and baggage of my life in the church.

It would possibly make a more interesting story to tell, had I one day woken up and made a conscious decision to leave the group. I would love to tell you I threw in the towel and assaulted the judgmental hierarchy with a string of profanities. But like many changes in life that lack courage, decisive choice, and vision, this came to me gradually, without really taking notice of it and with no real plan for what was to come. What I did notice was how difficult it was becoming to maintain my life day-to-day. Often at night I would awaken, hyper vigilant and alert from anxiety, convinced someone was going to harm us, and then in the daylight hours I felt like an elephant was standing on my chest from the pit of depression I had fallen into. I found myself drinking more and more often, which for a time helped with the anxiety and my never-ending fear-based thoughts. It helped me sleep when rest resisted. It did not, however, help with the loneliness I felt. A loneliness that today I know was rooted in a lack of being whole myself, and of not understanding my true nature. In the absence of this understanding, I had no inner peace or serenity.

Because of my lifestyle of drinking and eventually Cocaine and other drugs, I was disfellowshipped and shunned by the Witnesses and my family. But my belief that Armageddon was near remained, and I lived with certainty that I was not worthy of a place in this Universe and I would soon lose my life when it came.

Nine

Sometimes Love is Not Enough

It was 10 p.m. on a Friday night. As I walked through the entrance, the door guy held out his hand and quickly shook mine as he parted the rope letting me pass by the line of people who were waiting to be let in. The base thumped a quick techno beat and the lights and lasers flashed in the dark club. This club had become my refuge from the insanity in my head. On a couch to my right sat two girls, their pupils like saucers, while someone flashed glow sticks in front of their eyes to the beat of the music. Here I could ignore the idea that I was no longer a Witness and would die at Armageddon. I had grown into the religion and held its beliefs for many years since childhood. The pressure of a life of mind control had become too much for me though, and so over the last couple of years I had drifted away from it, first by drinking more and more and then by gradually adding different drugs to the mix in an attempt to control the noise in my head and numb the beliefs I had acquired. In this place, I could drink and hang out with other people who seemed to be happy.

I walked to the bar, ordered a drink and sat down. I looked around for "the guy," a twenty-something Vietnamese kid who always had the best Ecstasy. When I spotted him halfway across the room, I caught his eye and gave him a nod. We both headed to the bathroom where I bought five little blue pills with the image of a dolphin pressed into them for $20 apiece. I crushed the first one with my back teeth before swallowing. It was bitter and made me gag a little as I washed it down and rinsed my teeth with my drink. I pocketed the rest for later. If I spaced them out correctly, I would be able to peak longer and not take so much that I felt anxious, sweaty, and weird. Forty-five minutes later, I sat on a couch with a bottle of water in my hand. The familiar body roll had started. Wave after wave engulfed me. I felt completely at ease and relaxed, everyone and everything around me felt correct. The ever-present feeling of being ill at ease was gone. I was comfortable in my own skin. The night didn't end until long after the bars were closed and the sun was coming up as the multiple hits of Ecstasy were wearing off and the terrible sound of birds could be heard beginning to sing for a day's start that I had already wasted.

That was a typical Friday or Saturday night for me for a long time. As I pontificated to people the benefits of MDMA and regularly used 5-10 hits in a single night, my brain slowly depleted itself of serotonin. On days following heavy use, I felt dulled. My vocabulary seemed to lessen. Words that once were there were no longer accessible. I noticed this, and I didn't care. Before long, cocaine was introduced to the party. Where ecstasy made me feel less self-conscious and at ease, cocaine turned me into the most confident self-assured person on the planet. The moment I did my first line, I should have known how dangerous it was. But instead it felt like it was made for me. The escalation of use and the nose-dive in my life was rapid. Before long, coke became a daily necessity and I began selling it to support my habit. When snorting it just wasn't enough, someone suggested rocking it up, in other words making crack and smoking it, and I said, "sure why not?" What did I have to lose? Armageddon would be upon us any day and I was going to die anyway. Repeat that scene hundreds and hundreds of times and this became my life. The rest of the world continued. Armageddon didn't come, and I had become a drunk and a cokehead with no self-worth, hurting the people around me, and without the tools to be anything else.

On a rainy night in the fall, I sat in the passenger seat of a friend's car as we rode into a bad neighborhood. We pulled up and stopped in front of Butch, my Crack dealer's, house. I wouldn't have brought another person here except my friend had cash to buy with, and I had long since been broke, hustling wherever I could to support my habit. "Ok, give me the cash and wait here," I said. "I'll give it to you, but I'm coming with you," he replied. "Dude, you don't know what this guy is like, he'll be pissed if I take you in there," I pleaded. He insisted and I relented.

I knocked on the door of the garage that sat beneath the house and someone rolled it open from the inside. There were three guys sitting around a makeshift plywood table playing cards. All three were wearing Crips colors. Butch, a rough-looking black guy in his 50s, stood in the corner. The door rolled shut behind us as Butch glared at me. I had been here many times but hadn't ever brought anyone else. Butch and I walked together through a door into the house and into a bedroom. "Close that door!" He shouted at me. I could tell he wasn't happy. *Fuck why did I do this?* I thought as I turned to close the door.

We were standing in a dirty bedroom; the bed was unmade with a nasty looking blanket crumpled on it. There were boxes of junk sitting around. The worn-out carpet was filthy; it smelled like stale smoke and the dim light bulb in the fixture made the room feel small and dismal. I had smoked rock in this room dozens of times before. I could still hear the people talking in the other room a few feet away, but I couldn't take my eyes off of the sawed-off shotgun he held pointed at my chest. "Why the fuck you bring that white boy to my fucking house mother fucker?" He yelled. It wasn't the only time I had had a gun pointed at me, but this time I thought I was going to die. It became apparent that he was high and very paranoid.

Again, I felt like I was watching this scenario take place. I wasn't in my body; I observed it off to the side. I'm not sure what I said, but I stayed calm. Growing up with chaos had taught me to remain calm. Panic was trained out of me early when confronted with the potential of violence. Gradually, he calmed down and lowered the gun and with a pit in my stomach we completed our transaction so I could get high.

I still today believe I came extremely close to losing my life that night.

A few weeks later, I found myself facing the death of my father. After he died, I returned to the drug and alcohol treatment center and completed the 28-day inpatient program. I left there believing cocaine was a problem and an addiction. I had lied to myself about this for a very long time, so this was a milestone. But I continued the belief that alcohol was not in the same category as cocaine. I also left with a new group of associates to lean on. This brought with it its own set of problems. Now sort of sober, I was hanging out with people who were, like me, brand new to sobriety. It wasn't long before, rather than seeing each other in support groups, we began to see each other socially and from there it was an easy step back into my life of alcohol and drugs.

I believe this is a common misstep for any number of unhealthy behaviors a person is trying to overcome. It's evidence of the quote from Jim Rohn, *You're the average of the five people you spend the most time with.*[1] Not that I'm blaming any of those people for my behavior. Rather the quote speaks to social norms and what is acceptable within a group. I was most certainly also one of their five people. I believe this is

---

1   Rohn, Jim. "'Idaho Farm Boy Makes It to Beverly Hills." Speech, n.d.

one pitfall that can be found in 12-step groups if a person is not careful. You must choose not only the particular group, but also the individuals, wisely due to the culture you will surround yourself with. If you are looking for a support group to overcome any bad habit, make sure the culture of the group is based on positive behaviors that replace that bad habit. Some groups do little more than talk about the problem itself instead of the solution. And that goes against a principle that is at the very core of change. "What we resist persists." If we are trying to change something yet spending much of our time thinking about and talking about the thing we want to change, we are resisting it instead of replacing the thoughts and conversations with a vision of something better. In looking for support, I should have been seeking out people who were primarily talking about a solution, not dwelling on the problem itself. It seems amazingly simple, but it's key in changing our behaviors.

My life continued down this path for almost 20 years. It's an all too familiar story of addiction, rehab, recovery and return to addiction. I was divorced during that time from Connie with whom I had my first daughter. I cleaned up for a while because of the light my daughter brought to my world. If you are a parent, I don't need to describe to you the incredible love this brings to your life. There isn't a love that I have ever felt more deeply than what I feel for my children. Yet *even that* wasn't enough. It must be exceedingly difficult for the family of an addict or alcoholic to realize that no amount of love is enough to make a family member whole. Shortly after she was born, I entered drug treatment yet again and this time managed to more or less end my drug use. But I continued with the belief that alcohol wasn't a problem. I would go through periods of time when, because of pressure from other people, I would slow down but binge drinking always remained.

It was during one of these slower periods of time that I met Michaelle the love of my life, and two more wonderful people I have had the privilege to call my daughters, Gabrielle and Mary. Michaelle and I fell in love and were married. As we blended our two families into one, I began to see a much brighter future than I had ever allowed myself before. Yet booze continued to return. I sabotaged both my happiness and my family's happiness over and over. What I had always claimed was not a problem with alcohol but only an addiction to cocaine, even bragging about how I had "overcome addiction" became an even more full-blown issue using plain old vodka. I would swear it off one day and be back to it the next

While I worked and built a career in telecommunications sales, I progressed over several years to drinking more than a fifth of vodka each day and battled the same fundamental emotional problems I always had. As my family life began to decline because of my drinking, my career strangely prospered. Since my mom had instilled in me a strong work ethic and I had learned how to sell while knocking on doors for The Watchtower, I found a niche where my skills became prosperous and at the same time I found an environment where heavy drinking after work, at company events and on work-sponsored trips seemed not only acceptable, but normal. (In retrospect the way I acted was actually a stark contrast to most of the people around me.) Seemingly without effort, I had manifested the ideal reality to make excuses for the way I buried my problems in a bottle. I reached a point where I had all the things, I believed should make a person happy: a wife, family, career, travel, and money. But I was not happy. I was miserable and always anxious and my drinking continued to progress.

Shortly before "waking up," this is what a typical day was like for me. There were many of these, but this is the gist of what my life had become.

8 a.m. on an August morning: I was driving down the interstate on my morning commute toward the office. I had my cruise set on a steady 75 mph, just enough over the speed limit so I wouldn't look suspicious, but not so fast that I would get pulled over. As I poured the second or third shot of vodka into my coffee cup and slugged it down, I passed a state trooper in the right lane. I was driving a nice luxury SUV, so he didn't give me a second glance. My wife and children knew I drank far too much. I would show up at home every evening in a state I called "a little buzzed." but they certainly knew better than I admitted to myself how out of control I was. The truth is I couldn't remember the last time I spent even one full day without alcohol. It had become, I thought, my only means of keeping my sanity. If I were honest with myself I would have known I was more and more insane

in my thoughts and actions every day. When I arrived at the office, I was still nervous and jittery even though I had already drunk more than most people would on a night out.

By 11 a.m. I couldn't stand the discomfort anymore, so I feigned leaving to go on a "sales appointment." I went to my usual bar where I would meet up with a crowd who would drink with me for the rest of the day. People came and went. I was always there. That was the extent of my existence. This was every day of my life. I was robbing endless hours from my family and cheating the people I worked with. I couldn't remember when my chest didn't hurt on a regular basis, or when I ate a normal meal without vomiting. A day did not pass when my wife and I didn't fight or talk of divorce, when I didn't see disappointment and anxiety in the eyes of my children. This was not the life I ever imagined. I laughed and made jokes. I was the life of this horribly sad and destructive party for a long time, while I was dying inside and hurting everyone I cared about. I had become the husband and father I swore I never would. I could not find a way out. I would try to stop and swear I was not going to drink again and almost immediately go back. I was hopeless, afraid and thought I was completely alone.

It had to be terrifying, heartbreaking, infuriating, confusing, and humiliating to be my wife and children. As I look back, I am filled with gratitude that Michaelle and my children are still with me. Their story is just that: theirs. And that is why I haven't written about them in greater detail here. Perhaps one day my wife and I will write a book together.

There is certainly a need for help navigating family relationships before and in sobriety. What I can say with certainty is that without my family I would not be alive today. They deserved much better than I gave to them through those years.

This story is not meant to be comprehensive, but to show a picture of how addiction and alcoholism progressed in my life, and to paint a picture of some of the influences that formed me. As well as to give credence to the idea that due to my history, I understand what it takes to change and to transform a life. All too often addiction recovery stories fall into recounting every horrible deed that transpired. For me, I believe to do that would be based in an "I was a worse drunk than anyone else" form of ego or "I had it harder than anyone else" type of excuse making. I do not believe that. I certainly hope I have not painted that picture. Many people have stories much more difficult than mine and don't turn to this sort of behavior. I was blessed with some things that others never get to experience, like feeling loved by my parents, having an example of a strong work ethic from my mom and having a wife and children in my life who didn't give up on me when they probably should have. I am grateful each and every day for those things.

Addiction is tricky to the addict. In my own mind, addiction to drugs and alcohol seemed controlled at times and then other times it would sneak up on me and take that control away. Though in retrospect, because of the image I had of my father, a lack of self-worth, being taught I didn't have a place in this Universe if I didn't earn it, and having no autonomy for my own life's vision and choices, I developed a way of surviving where I continually went back and forth between running away from things I had an aversion to and craving things I desired. There was no middle ground. Like many people, I had mistaken pleasure for happiness. I was like a wood pile soaked in gasoline. Drugs and alcohol were the lit match. Setting it ablaze was the easy part of my life. It took no courage at all and the habits I fell into took no effort. Waking up and continuing to change and grow as a person while building a better character is the more difficult part. Yet as difficult as it is at times, it is also the most rewarding and wonderful experience I can imagine. To get to become a whole person and be on a path of discovery each day brings a richness to life that is immeasurable. The following chapters are where my life really began.

Part Two

THE BIG BLOCKS

OF CHANGE

Ten

Waking Up

As I checked into rehab for the third time, I was a broken person. My drinking had continued to increase. I was detoxing from a fifth and a half of vodka every day. The first few minutes standing there with my wife who, despite her better judgment had stuck with me, I felt a sense of relief. The last several years were like a bad carnival ride that I couldn't seem to get off of.

Franky, the intake coordinator showed us to his office where someone collected my bag taking it to another room to be searched for drugs or other contraband. "Would you like me to show you the facility, Mrs. Gallagher?" He asked. She declined, and we said our goodbyes. As she walked away, selfishly I felt abandoned and alone. She seemed to walk out without a glance backward. I think she was probably relieved and very tired. I had put my family through hell.

"Have you drank or used today?" Franky asked. "Not today. I wanted to, but I wanted to show up sober," I replied. "When was the last time?" He probed. "Yesterday into last night," I admitted. Franky laughed. "Just one last time huh?" I smiled a little. I think he was trying to make me feel at ease. He was a recovering addict himself. He told me about the multiple treatments he had gone through. One treatment program was an entire year. After which he went into a sober living house for two more. I started to like him. He seemed genuine and I thought maybe I could get something out of this. I had a slight glimmer of hope start to form in those first few moments.

"Have you eaten today?" he asked. "I can't remember. I think I had something this morning," I replied. "Come with me. I'll show you the common area and see if we can find you something to eat. Then the doctor or one of the nurses will meet with you to decide if you need any medications to detox. Based on how much you've been drinking I think they will probably recommend that." He led me first to a small room where I had to pee in a cup for him and perform a Breathalyzer. It was a routine I would repeat often while there. I was glad I hadn't lied about what would be in my system. He then took me to the common room that Michaelle and I had walked through upon entering, here I was deposited at a long row of tables next to the kitchen. The cook offered me a sandwich leftover from the lunch that had been served an hour or so before I arrived. I declined. Franky excused himself, leaving me to my new environment. Other patients walked past, some talking to one another, some keeping to themselves. A couple of them said hello. It felt like the first day of school, but I had shown up with an unbelievably bad hangover and the shakes.

By the time the nurse was able to see me, the tremors in my hands that I had been hiding with a drink first thing in the morning were visible to her. She had something for me to sign and I couldn't hold the pen still enough to write my name. She took my blood pressure, checked my temperature and listened to my heart and lungs. Then she said, "From what you've told me, I believe the doctor will want to prescribe a medicine to assist you in detoxing from the alcohol. How do you feel about that?" I had no objections. She left the room and came back a few minutes later with a prescription for Librium. Librium is a brand name for Chlordiazepoxide. It is a sedative and hypnotic medication used to treat withdrawal from alcohol. Alcohol withdrawal can be quite dangerous causing a long list of severe symptoms even the possibility of death.

"We will give you this for seven days. We will gradually reduce the dosage each day. It will lessen the risk of seizures and will help with your comfort as you withdraw," the nurse told me. She handed me a small paper cup with two pills in it along with a triangular funnel for the water dispenser. I swallowed the pills. She showed me the schedule and highlighted times when I should come to her office for medicine each day: morning, noon and night.

I was taken to the room that I would share with another guy. As I entered, I saw that my bag was open and my belongings were strewn across my bed. I started to fold the few clothes I had and then picked up the photo of my girls that I had brought with me. As I looked at their faces a tear dropped from my eye into the middle of it. *How did I end up here again?* I wondered to myself. Then everything began to feel heavy like I was trying to move or swim through Jell-O. The Librium was kicking in.

The next seven days felt like I was in a hypnotic sleep. It was as if I existed underwater, weaving my way through the hallways to nurse appointments, counseling, and meals. That week was the only real sleep I got while I was there. The worst of that week was the second night. As I began to detox from the large amount of alcohol my body and brain had become accustomed to, hallucinations started. At one point I believed my roommate, a kind, soft-spoken guy, was a vampire trying to kill me. He appeared above my bed with a demonic face and fangs. I ran screaming from the room and curled up in the corner of the common area with my back against the wall.

I recall speaking to my family on the phone through that week but have no idea what we talked about. The medicine had me completely zoned out. When my wife and three older daughters came to visit the following Saturday, they reported to me later that I didn't recognize them. As they walked through the door, I looked up at them and then went back to coloring a picture. I am sure that must have been traumatic for my family, like I was some sort of asylum-style lunatic who had been drugged into submission. Finally, at the end of the medicinal detox period, the Librium was withdrawn and my faculties began to return. It was then that I came to realize just what I had gotten into.

Having been raised in a spiritually abusive religion, by this time I had become an atheist. Or maybe agnostic without a belief in the spirit world. My cult religious upbringing carried with it the effects of trauma and post-traumatic stress disorder (PTSD) symptoms. I regularly awoke in the night screaming, convinced I was being attacked by Satan and demons. Even with no belief in the supernatural, these symptoms persisted throughout my adult life. Twelve-step programs continuously preached a higher power and God so I wanted nothing to do with that. And as someone who needed to see the science behind something, I didn't believe the 12 steps could help me. In my mind, the conformity also smacked a bit of cultishness. Because of these feelings I had sought out a treatment facility that did not use a 12-step approach and I was assured a number of times that any religious portions of the program were only there for people who wanted that in their recovery. This was based on science and cognitive behavioral therapy. I came to find out that was not the reality.

The program was founded in Catholicism, which surprisingly did not bother me if I could opt out of any religion in my treatment plan. In practice, all the Catholic teachings and dogma had been stripped from the program except for allowing patients to attend mass if they chose to do so. It was replaced, however, by a culture of extreme fundamental evangelical Christianity. The lectures often began on a note of secular ethics and then descended into preaching tirades about the power of the Holy Ghost. I came to find out that around 75 percent of the staff attended the same fundamentalist church together.

It's my opinion that their hierarchy of what needed to take place was something like:

1. Conversion to their form of Christianity.
2. Religious counseling.
3. And only after the above two happened did they focus on treatment of addiction through traditional psychological counseling.

Because of my history, the nonstop talk of the devil and his part in addiction was a major trigger for the PTSD symptoms I had previously experienced. My nightmares of being attacked by the devil and demons increased. Whenever I would fall asleep, I would wake up in a sweat screaming. I think my mental state probably made my roommate very uncomfortable. But I hung in there, genuinely wanting to be well. I also could not bear to let my family down again. I had walked in the door broken and feeling dead in so many ways. I was determined to get better.

When I spoke to my counselor about the PTSD symptoms, I told him about the nightmares where I was attacked by demons and the devil. He told me that it was his belief that PTSD was nothing more than an attack by the enemy and should be regarded as such. He then attempted once again to convince me of the need to become a believer. The rules of the unit were that by 11 p.m., all patients were to return to their rooms and stay there until 5 a.m. barring an emergency. Being unable to sleep and having terrifying nightmares made this an awful experience. Sharing a room made it impossible to do anything but lay in the dark unable to sleep. I spent night after night like this after hearing far too many references to fear-based religion and almost no counseling to get to the root of my problems. This, along with the nightmares when I did fall asleep, took its toll on my already fragile grasp of not giving up. I began crying almost incessantly. The other patients could be helpful and encouraging, but overall, the program sent me to the edge of insanity. My mind continuously came back to the thought of taking my own life. I pictured it over and over, along with other racing thoughts with little organization or construction. It was just continuous fear-based thoughts that would not stop. It became too much to bear. Finally, in this state of despair and fear, one night I stole a sharp knife from the kitchen and carried it into the shower with me intending to cut my wrists. I didn't want to be dead, but I was so broken, alone and afraid I couldn't face another moment like this. I couldn't see another option. I broke into tears standing under the hot water, and as it ran over my head I slumped to the floor and sobbed and sobbed. It felt like a dam had broken and every terrible thing that was trapped inside came pouring out. I sobbed for my parents who had died. I sobbed because of who I had become as a father and over the damage I had caused my children. I sobbed over how I had treated my wife, the love of my life. I sobbed out of the hopelessness I felt and how out of control my own mind felt to me. I sobbed for my beautiful daughters who I so wanted to give a better life than I had been given, but instead I had shown them a drunk. I sobbed over my marriage that once felt like a fairy tale and was now lying in pieces. And I cried for myself over this disappointing life I had created. The same one that as a child I swore I never would. I stayed there sobbing until the water ran ice cold and a little longer, without following through with my plan.

My mind was still moving rapidly from one thought to the next. I don't think there was ever a moment in my life where I had felt at ease. Those moments that night were some of the worst though. There was no organization or construction to my thoughts, just continuous hopelessness that would not stop. After breaking down in the shower, I found myself dressed and walking. I didn't know exactly where I needed to go, I just knew I needed to be outdoors. I walked barefoot through the grass. It felt soft and cool under my feet. I was in a grassy field 50 yards or so from the main building. I sat on top of a picnic table under the very bright stars. I took some deep breaths trying to calm myself. My breathing slowed as I concentrated on only my breath in and out. In my hand I held the mala that had been sent to me, fingering one bead to the next and reciting my self-made mantra of, *I am calm, I am peace, I am love.* My breathing steadied some and my thoughts poured out into the Universe, completely genuine, completely bare and completely raw.

Help me! Please help me! I begged.

As I continued and time passed a complete calm came over me. I became alert to a moment of time, now, that I was a part of. The frenetic terror of hopelessness wasn't there. I was away from it, behind it somewhere. For the first time I could see who I really was, or rather who I was not. I was able to observe who I had always believed myself to be. I believe today it was a moment of transcendence and in that moment of calm transcendence, I changed. I felt at ease. I finally heard the message the Universe had been attempting to tell me: *You are not alone. You have a place here. You belong. You don't have to earn your place here; it is already yours.*

I felt to my innermost self a connection to everyone and everything surrounding me.. I felt a part of everything else. I realized that the voice that was always talking to me in my head, telling me I'm not enough, that I'm different, wasn't really me. That voice of ego was the thing that was in the way of knowing who I really am.

This change is what I refer to today as "waking up." In one moment, I felt broken, alone, terrified, hopeless, craving, and wishing to end my life. And the next moment I was a different human being. A psychic shift had taken place. I suddenly understood a connection to something larger and I knew I was a part of it. I had a place in it. I had a feeling of an unexplained energy that connects all of us and caught a glimpse of it.

I woke up the following morning and understood to my core and my innermost self that things would be ok. That I would be ok. My desire for drugs and alcohol was gone. The desire to be numb had vanished. And I have felt like an altogether different person since that night.

It's not lost on me the way that sounds. If I had heard someone say what I just wrote to you, I would have dismissed them as ignorant, or crazy or both. I would have laughed at the ridiculousness of it. All I have to offer you is anecdotal evidence of its truth. My life drastically changed in those moments and the moments since because a fundamental shift in my consciousness took place. It was as if I had spent my previous life asleep and now, I was awake.

Perhaps I had been shown grace or maybe the years of mental strain, trauma and chaos finally became too great and my brain shifted out of a sheer sense of survival. In trying to explain something I have no explanation for, the words of the Tao ring in my ears, *much speech leads inevitably to silence. Better to hold fast to the void.*[1]

Knowing my words cannot quite describe this, it is still my hope that my story and especially the methods I found to grow after this happened can help others enact change in their lives. Because waking up for me was just the first step. I still had a lot of work to do.

The methods I have used since that night to grow aren't new or my own, quite the opposite in fact. What I have seen and learned is that there are some very central themes, currents, and threads of truth within positive psychology, secular ethics, spiritual belief systems and even quantum physics. The threads they all have in common are the basic truths

---

1   Laozi, and D. C. Lau. *Tao Te Ching.* Harmondsworth: Penguin Books, 1963.

about the human condition. These truths are the primer, or basic education I needed, for happiness and inner peace. The night I woke up I touched on this reality of existence.

Eleven

Becoming a Student

It is my hope that my story so far has painted a picture of what led me to a life of alcoholism and addiction. I carried with me limiting beliefs, no sense of self, improper development and alignment of values and a lack of courage when faced with someone else's vision for me. I vacillated between running away from things that were uncomfortable and running toward things I craved. It was this foundation of aversion and attraction that I had first built my life upon that was the cause of my suffering. My story may be much different in its details than your story. Yet at the root of a great many problems lay the same foundations. That is why I can inform you with a certainty there is immense value in the tools I soon found that helped me transform my life.

Shortly after the night I woke up, I checked myself out of the rehab facility. Because of my newfound yet still slight understanding of my place in the Universe, I knew it was not the place for me. However, it is exceptionally difficult to explain a shift like this to family members who have witnessed the destructive effects of alcoholism and addiction. I did not quite understand the shift myself, to suddenly tell them I had "woken up" I'm sure would have made them think I simply wanted to be away from the place so I could drink again. So, I continued with another treatment program in an outpatient facility close to home to set my family's minds at ease. I felt I owed them that. I'm glad I did this. This not only helped reinforce my commitment to healing, but it also allowed me access to information I may not have had otherwise. The center was a dual-diagnosis program. What that means is that along with treatment of addiction it was also designed to help with emotional or mental health challenges. I learned about how others suffer with mental health issues and it helped me develop compassion for a group of people I would not have otherwise spent time with. I was able to understand more about anxiety and PTSD along with tools to help. I was also able to spend time with Gordy, my counselor. He is a wise man who gave me great advice and shared his own story with me in a very humble and kind way.

Waking up was just the beginning for me. I had a lifetime of bad habits, both in thinking and in actions that I needed to overcome. To understand how to change this lifetime repository of bad character, I became a student on the subject of transformation. I voraciously consumed everything I could within positive psychology, spiritual traditions, religion, and quantum physics.

By doing this, I gained what I believe is a fundamental understanding of my reality. I have come to believe that there is an energy that surrounds us, is in us, and that we are a part of. Since we are an expression of that energy, we have the choice of what we attract into our lives, both good and bad. Once I understood this, transformation could be more easily accomplished.

The following chapters are about some of the things I needed to develop in my character to live in alignment with this understanding and to build the foundational qualities necessary for success. These things are what I refer to as *Big Blocks of Change.* Just like when I walk my daughter through cleaning her room, after the big blocks there is always space for addition and refinement. I say this again about space for refinement because when writing a book about transformation and self-improvement a writer runs the risk of sounding preachy or painting the idea that he or she has perfected the method they propose. Nothing could be further from the truth in my case, or anyone else's really. This is a path I am walking and one I hope to continue always improving upon. I believe that personally, I will always have much to improve on. I see it every day. This, however, gives me tools and a direction as I improve. I can also say with confidence that my life is radically different today. The tools are courage, questioning our beliefs, aligning our values, learning, living in gratitude, and compassion along with a meditation practice.

Most are a part of wisdom traditions that are thousands of years old. And they are also backed up by modern science and medicine. These things have given me an inner peace and joy I did not imagine was possible. Perhaps you will find value in them as well.

Twelve

Fear, Courage and What Lies Beyond

There's a great scene near the beginning of the movie *Joe Versus The Volcano*. If you haven't seen this movie, you absolutely should. It's a great story about waking up. To set the scene for you, Joe, the hypochondriac main character played by Tom Hanks, is returning to work after yet another appointment with the doctor. This time, though, the doctor has told him he's going to die. He walks back into his dreary office with gray walls, terrible fluorescent lights buzzing overhead, and half-dead looking people to confront his boss, Mr. Waturi. In the process of collecting his things and walking out of this awful situation, Joe goes into a monologue directed at Mr. Waturi, where he, in colorful language, questions why he has put up with this existence in misery for so long doing work *he probably could have done in six months*. And then he answers his own question. He says, "Fear! Yellow freaking fear! I've been too afraid to live my life, so I sold it to you for 300 freaking dollars a week!"

Why Do We Limit Ourselves?

It is my belief that we must question what is motivating the drive or lack of drive to attain the greatness that is already inside of us. Energy and success sit waiting for us to tap into. I propose that when we choose to limit ourselves, it is almost always based in fear. So, while discussing how to wake up and transform, it becomes particularly important to discuss fear and one of its antidotes, courage.

As I write this, the world is gripped in fear, possibly more than usual. Covid-19 has isolated us from our social circles, our normal work environments, friends, and extended family. As the world sits behind closed doors and wears masks to keep the virus at bay, it is becoming sicker and sicker with the insidious disease of fear. It's on a 24-hour news cycle. We are bombarded with the number of cases, the number of deaths and the uncertainty of life right now. We ask ourselves, "Will someone I love become sick from it? Will my parents, will my children, will my spouse, will I?" Not to mention the anxiety of the economy. "Will I continue to have a job? Will I lose my retirement?" The list goes on. All of that is in addition to the normal anxieties and fears our society was already crippled with before the outbreak: poor health, finances, children, family problems, workload and performance, death, social phobias, etc.

I find this subject extremely interesting, because it has made such a huge impact on my life.

Fear was a major a part of my existence since early childhood. On a physical level, I was often afraid of whether we would have enough to eat and whether we would have a place to live, or if the police would be at the door that day to arrest my father. Would we be thrown on the floor that night by my dad because he thought someone driving past may shoot at our house? Some of those were very real fears. Because of the criminal life my father lived, he was shot in the back of the head in 1980 while fleeing an armed robbery. I was eight years old and I found out about it along with my mom on the evening news. That was a very real fear realized. Then there were the mental fears that were taught to me by the cult and I came to accept. I think these were worse. I was afraid that any day Armageddon would come, the government would kick in our door put us in prison and then they would torture us to break us of our faith. With that limiting belief system, I was almost always afraid of something. I was taught at a very primal level to be afraid of Satan and his demons, wicked spirits who God would allow to attack me if I wasn't doing his work. This was completely real to me even into early adulthood. Even after leaving those beliefs behind, I would regularly wake up at night from nightmares, screaming in a cold sweat. Even my children knew not to try to shake me awake but to say my name from across the room because I came out of bed swinging.

So, when I examined transformation, fear was such a huge part of me that finding an antidote to it became paramount. As we've discussed, for me, the two major things that held me back were a mind controlling religion and addiction. Walking away from the religion of my youth involved loss. The religion practices shunning former members who choose to no longer be a part of it. They call this "disfellowshipping." I had to face the loss of my entire circle of friends, and people who felt like family. And I had to face the loss of my actual family. Once I left the religion, my mom, brothers and extended family all cut me off. We no longer spent time together, talked on the phone, or exchanged emails. Absolutely every form of association ended. It makes me sad that my mom held these beliefs until she died, and that my closest friend and brother, Gary, still does. This loss was coupled with my firm belief at the time that the religion was still true and right. That I was walking away from God. That decision had a great deal of fear behind it. And I didn't walk away easily. The Universe kept calling. I fought depression and addiction through it and because of it. Before I left, I attempted suicide twice. Until finally it was forced upon me. I was disfellowshipped and I HAD to face the realization of all those fears. The Universe dragged me through that door.

Do you remember earlier when I said I feel lucky today to have experienced the shitty, rotten stuff I went through? It's not because I'm a masochist or a martyr, but it's because without it, without addiction, ending up down and out, homeless, helpless and alone, I probably wouldn't have

had the *courage* to leave the comfort of what I had alw
believed. Because even when our reality is awful, it's just that:
our reality. It's what is normal to us. It is what has always
been. So, walking into something different seems so hard.
It's scary. We're often taught that people fear the unknown.
I don't believe that. I believe they fear the *loss* of the known.
In a very literal way that was me. I wasn't afraid so much of
living a life different than the one the church allowed us to
live. That life was awful. But I was very afraid of the loss of
the known. I was afraid of the loss of my friends, the only
sense of stability I had known, and being a part of my family's
lives. The loss of being able to watch my nieces and nephews
grow up. It's a very scary thing to be alone. And I didn't have
the courage to do that outright at the time. I hadn't developed
courage to stand up and say to a spiritually abusive hierarchy,
*this is bullshit! You are not going to control my life any longer, I
want more than this. I exist for more than this! I am more than
this! And I have a lot more to offer than this!*

Instead I walked through that door kicking and screaming and trying to hide. I was using mind-altering substances
to look anywhere except the pain and reality of that change.
Then when addiction reared its head and became full-blown
in my life, I was backed into a corner again and faced with
change. I came awfully close to hiding again. I contemplated
suicide again because I was so broken and afraid to face what
I had become. I was afraid to face what using drugs and
alcohol had turned my life into. But instead I faced it.

A Reward for Courage

The first real courage I showed in my life was the moment I was completely vulnerable and said to my wife, "I need help." I had denied that I had a problem to everyone else because it was so scary to say it out loud. Saying it out loud would make it real and hold me responsible to change, to give up the only coping mechanism I had found. For so long I denied it to my wife, friends, family and people I worked with. But deep down inside I knew. If you're dealing with addiction somewhere inside you know. You know how big the problem really is. We just deny it so often to everyone that we sort of believe it ourselves. But deep down somewhere we know.

A while back, a mentor asked me about my life today. "Fill in this blank for me," he said, "life is _____." As I sat and thought about it, the only word I could use to describe it was, "beautiful." Life is beautiful!

And there is the rub between fear and courage. If we are courageous, on the other side of facing our fears, there is beauty!

That's what life is for me today. It's beautiful. It's not perfect, but it's beautiful. I wake up in the morning and get to learn something new. My mind is not controlled any longer by someone telling me what I can and cannot think about. You see freedom of thought is somewhat taken for granted and because of that, it's not utilized to the degree it should be. I can tell you from personal experience that to have it taken from you, to have your mind and actions controlled, is not something to take for granted. Drugs and alcohol do the same thing. Today they do not inhabit my brain space even for a moment. I get to look at my children and not see looks of disappointment. I can look my wife in the eye without feeling guilt and shame. An entirely different world has opened to me. The wonder of all that surrounds us jumps out almost every moment of the day. I have the privilege of seeing the world with a child's eyes. Something I didn't even get to do when I was a child. That's the reward for me in finding courage. That's the reward for facing fear. I get to live in agreement with the energy of the Universe, instead of fighting it.

I think it's also important to note that the first step in courage isn't necessarily an action. It's an intention. You're committing to the action, saying it to yourself and sharing it with others. (And you can do this even if you don't quite believe it yourself yet.) When I committed to the action of overcoming addiction, I said it out loud to a few people I am close to. That was scary. I don't know what I expected but the warmth and support I received from my wife, Michaelle, my children, and from my friends, Cameron, Shane, Shawn and Brendan was entirely unexpected and wonderful. It made a huge difference in my resolve to change. When I made myself vulnerable enough to share that intention, it made it a little easier to take the next step and then the next one. It also made me accountable. I walked across that bridge throwing matches behind me. After I told others my intention, I could not go back. That was terrifying. But there was courage in it.

The situation may be different for you. You may be battling with something completely different than I did. Your reward for being courageous and making change may be yet unknown. But deep down I believe we all know the choice that needs to be made.

With the big, important things, sometimes we get lucky enough that the Universe drags us through that door as it did to me several times, before I heard the message behind it. But at some point, somewhere sometime to get to the beauty and reward, we *have to be courageous.*

We have to say to ourselves, *yes I'm afraid, but I'm going to do it anyway. I want something different!* Change is scary. Change hurts. When we change, we will lose something. But I assure you there is beauty and wonder and reward on the other side of it.

Courage was the first "Big Block of Change" that I discovered.

Thirteen

What if Michelangelo Was a Plumber?

So, it has become apparent that courage is involved in transformation. The next thing I realized as I searched in the many
books I was reading and from what I was learning from my
mentors was just how limiting my beliefs were and how they
were holding me back. However, I never would have seen this
if I hadn't questioned them. When my family and friends in
the church shunned me as they were directed, I still believed
the teachings. We have already discussed mind control and
how that's the head space I was in. Even though today I view
this as a gift in disguise, at the time, it was heartbreaking and
frightening. For a little while before I woke up, I considered
trying to return to the church asking to be accepted back
into the fold because of this heartbreak. Then one particularly difficult day my wife asked me a question. "If the church
someday disfellowshipped Emma (my daughter who was 5 at

the time), would you shun her and not have her as a part of your life?" That question was like the first small hole in the dam. The belief system I had adopted did not allow me to question the authority of the church's teachings. I hadn't even questioned the possibility that it was wrong for my family and friends to shun me since the Witnesses went so far as to equate questioning the teachings of the Watchtower as apostate and what the bible refers to as an unforgivable sin.

That question my wife asked sat with me for quite some time, returning to my mind over and over. No matter how I looked at it, I couldn't imagine ever shunning one of my children over *anything*. Before long, I was questioning other things and then more until one after another, brick by brick, the wall of mind control crumbled because I began questioning my beliefs.

Develop the Habit of Questioning Beliefs

Cult mind control is a very extreme example of the way our beliefs can be limiting. However, when we examine the beliefs that drive our actions is it that different for any of us? Many times, we are not an active participant in our acquired beliefs, and we don't question them. The path we choose is often chosen for us before we're able to be a part of the choice. Our parents do this, our culture does this, our religions do this. Until we become an active participant in questioning our beliefs and coming to conclusions on our own, we are largely following someone else's path and we've adopted someone else's values. A kid may adopt the belief that law school is the path for him because it has been the path for his parents. He may accept that belief and expectation. That decision, though, can be the enemy of happiness. What if Michelangelo's parents taught him the value of becoming a plumber and he never questioned that belief? We would not have the Sistine Chapel. What if Albert Einstein was encouraged to stay on the path of working in a patent office, and he listened to that? Science would be greatly stunted. The Sagrada Familia isn't a practical piece of architecture. But it's beautiful. We wouldn't have it if Gaudi followed someone else's beliefs and values. To a kid living in the inner-city slinging rock on the corner may seem acceptable and deep down he may have been given a belief system that this is the best way forward without examining it. Yet until we start questioning those kinds of beliefs and building a value system of our own, instead of using someone else's values, we get someone else's dreams, someone else's vision, someone else's results, and someone else's life. To me this is not living in harmony with the energy of the Universe.

Every single human on this planet has something inside to offer. But you have to question your beliefs and find your own values. How many Michelangelo's, Einstein's and Gaudi's are stifled living with someone else's beliefs and values? Our industrial society loves the practical. The machine does not want you to question your belief about what is actually possible in your life. It needs cogs or it doesn't work, but to us as individuals and as people, adopting other's values, visions, and beliefs as our own without first questioning them hides our beauty. The mass hallucination we live under is that you are the cog, yet deep down you know you're not! So, question the belief that you are. While it is true the world needs janitors, that doesn't mean you have to be one of them.

That's not to say that there isn't a janitor who sees the beauty in what he does. Perhaps this occupation brings him or her closer to the Universe, not further away. That's tremendous! I'm not taking away the value of any profession or activity, I'm simply saying you have to question where the belief in your lifestyle comes from, and how it has molded your values. Are they your own? This is important because our beliefs and values dictate our vision and the course of our life, and ultimately our happiness.

Where Does Unhappiness Originate?

So, we've talked about the need for courage to walk through the fear of what we may lose. We've also talked about the power of questioning limiting beliefs. Let's talk briefly about values because it's important to be clear on what *our* values are so we know if we are living in alignment with them.

We all hold values and need values. They are a part of what makes a society successful and fulfilling. What was very eye opening to me when I examined myself is that *my frustration and unhappiness came almost entirely from not living in harmony with my own values or when I lived by the values of others.*

My own values of loyalty, creativity, and inner peace were in direct conflict with how I was living my life, both while

I was under the mind control of a cult, and after, when I used substances to numb and dull my discomfort. Because my values and my actions were incongruent, almost nothing seemed to be fulfilling. This became noticeably clear to me when I completed the following exercise. Take a few minutes to do this exercise because clarifying our core values can be rather eye opening and is a great tool in designing the life we want because it changes our behavior.

CORE VALUES

EXERCISE

The First part of this exercise is to take a few minutes to think about what qualities are important to you. This is difficult for some people. A good way to get in touch with it is to try to remember experiences or times when you felt a great deal of contentment or fulfillment. What was happening when you felt that way? What were you doing? What were the values involved in those situations?

Now go through the list provided below and circle 20 of the values that are most important to you as an individual. If you think of something that is not on the list, that's fine, write it down.

Accountability	Communication	Dependability	Family
Accuracy	Community	Determination	Famous
Achievement	Compassion	Development	Fearless
Adaptability	Competence	Devotion	Fidelity
Altruism	Concentration	Dignity	Focus
Ambition	Confidence	Discipline	Foresight
Amusement	Connection	Discovery	Fortitude
Bravery	Consciousness	Drive	Freedom
Brilliance	Consistency	Effectiveness	Friendship
Calm	Contentment	Efficiency	Fun
Candor	Contribution	Empathy	Generosity
Capable	Control	Empower	Genius
Careful	Conviction	Endurance	Giving
Certainty	Cooperation	Energy	Goodness
Challenge	Courage	Enjoyment	Grace
Charity	Courtesy	Enthusiasm	Gratitude
Cleanliness	Creation	Equality	Greatness
Clear	Creativity	Ethical	Growth
Clever	Credibility	Excellence	Happiness
Comfort	Curiosity	Experience	Hard work
Commitment	Decisiveness	Expressive	Harmony
Common sense	Dedication	Fairness	Health

Honesty	Passion	Smart	Winning
Honor	Patience	Solitude	Wisdom
Hope	Peace	Spirit	Wonder
Humility	Performance	Spirituality	Reliability
Humor	Persistence	Spontaneous	Open-
Imagination	Playfulness	Stability	mindedness
Improvement	Poise	Status	Good humor
Independence	Potential	Stewardship	Spirit of
Individuality	Power	Strength	adventure
Inner Peace	Present	Structure	Positivity
Innovation	Productivity	Success	Fitness
Inquisitive	Professionalism	Support	Education
Insightful	Prosperity	Surprise	Perseverance
Inspiring	Purpose	Sustainability	Patriotism
Integrity	Quality	Talent	Service to
Intelligence	Realistic	Teamwork	others
Intensity	Reason	Temperance	Environmen-
Intuitive	Reflective	Thankful	talism
Joy	Respect	Thorough	
Justice	Responsibility	Thoughtful	
Kindness	Restraint	Timeliness	
Knowledge	Results-oriented	Tolerance	
Lawful	Reverence	Toughness	
Leadership	Rigor	Traditional	
Learning	Risk	Tranquility	
Liberty	Satisfaction	Transparency	
Logic	Security	Trust	
Love	Self-reliance	Trustworthy	
Loyalty	Selfless	Truth	
Mastery	Sensitivity	Understanding	
Maturity	Serenity	Uniqueness	
Meaning	Service	Unity	
Moderation	Sharing	Valor	
Motivation	Significance	Victory	
Openness	Silence	Vigor	
Optimism	Simplicity	Vision	
Order	Sincerity	Vitality	
Organization	Skill	Wealth	
Originality	Skillfulness	Welcoming	

The next steps are where this exercise becomes a bit more difficult. Now you must eliminate 10 from the list of 20 leaving only the 10 that are the most important to you. Write them below.

1.   6.
2.   7.
3.   8.
4.   9.
5.   10.

Now eliminate 5 more leaving only 5 and write them below. This can be tough. Remember though that by eliminating one from this list you aren't eliminating it from your life, or labeling yourself. We all have a lot more than 5, 10, or 20 values we live with. And our values can certainly change over time. This is just an exercise to help us to see which ones are our own and most important right now so we can align our actions with them.

1.
2.
3.
4.
5.

Now, if you can, eliminate 2 more narrowing your list to just 3.

1.
2.
3.

Was that difficult? Eye Opening? Frustrating? It has been all those things for me each time I have done it.

Now write down a few ways in the past that by NOT acting in alignment with these core values you have felt unfulfilled or unhappy. Don't make this about beating yourself up, just get a sense of where they weren't present before, and how this may have been involved in a feeling of discontent or unhappiness.

And finally, with these 3 core values in mind write a paragraph or two for yourself below, expressing how these values can serve you. A few areas to analyze might be, in your relationships, how you think about yourself, or in your career choices. They literally can touch every aspect of your life.

If our actions are not living up to our own inner self, we aren't living in harmony with the energy we are a part of, and we cannot help but be unhappy. Why not take some time to ponder how your core values are lining up to your everyday activities? By doing this, the changes we need to make begin coming into focus.

Questioning beliefs and aligning core values were the next 'Big Blocks of Change' that I encountered.

Fourteen

How to Live in a Constant State of Amazement

Another one of my favorite quotes from *Joe Versus The Volcano* comes from one of the characters played by Meg Ryan. In this particular scene, Joe is becoming awestruck by what he's waking up to. He's speaking to her about how unbelievable her life seems to him and she says to him, "My Father says that almost the whole world is asleep, everybody you know, everybody you see, everybody you talk to. He says that only a few people are awake, and they live in a state of constant amazement." She's right! Some people do walk around continuously amazed and awestruck by this life we have. I certainly feel that way today. One of the biggest things that awakens this sense of amazement is learning. The more we learn, the more we realize how much we don't know. That probably sounds simple. You may think, *I have heard this before.* And you would be right. But it does not make it less true. We can become so wrapped up in our own viewpoint and ego that we stop learning and lose our curiosity and sense of wonder.

As children, we are little sponges soaking up experience and knowledge at an unbelievable rate. Biologically, children's brains develop rapidly, and they are able to learn very quickly. There may be a bit more to it though. They do not yet possess nearly as much of a false sense of self as adults do. They seem to have an innate understanding of a reality that we forget and a curiosity to learn more. When we grow up, we can lose much of that. We can see this referenced in most of the major spiritual traditions.

The Curiosity of a Child

In Christianity, when Jesus' disciples were keeping children away to not disturb him, he said, *Let the little children come to me, the kingdom of heaven belongs to such like ones.*[1] Lao Tzu in *The Tao Te Ching* asks, *Can you interact with the universal by staying soft and tranquil? Can you pursue the wisdom of Tao by discarding what you think you know?*[2]

And in Tibetan Buddhism there is a story that infants have a song they sing which goes something like, "Oh don't let me forget who I am." Then after growing up just a bit the child sings, "Oh please help me, I'm beginning to forget who I am."

1   Matthew 19:14. *The New Testament: New International Version.* Paulist Press, 1986.
2   Laozi, and D. C. Lau. *Tao Te Ching.* Harmondsworth: Penguin Books, 1963.

Even if you can't subscribe to the ideas of heaven or reincarnation, the principles here are beautiful. Somewhere along the way, most of us begin to develop an attitude of already knowing and understanding things. Our ego gets involved and we shut off that part of our minds to a large extent. We lose the wonder of learning and curiosity that a child so naturally has. I think all of us to some extent and on some level miss that feeling. We see it in stories, movies and books continuously. So how do we get it back? How do you turn learning, curiosity and wonder back into a habit?

Become a voracious reader! This is a habit that I believe is an essential aid in growth. It is one of the 'Big Blocks of Change' I began to incorporate. And I am in good company in this belief. There is a great story about Warren Buffett where he was asked about the key to success. He pointed to a stack of book in his office and said, "Read 500 pages like this every day. That's how knowledge works. It builds, like compound interest." It's said that Buffett devotes 80 percent of his day to reading! He may be an extreme example but he's also an extreme example of success. And he's not alone. Bill Gates reads at least 50 books a year. Mark Cuban reads more than three hours a day. Anthony Robbins calls reading one of the most valuable habits of his life. And I love this quote from Jim Rohn, *The difference between where you are today and where you'll be five years from now will be found in the quality of books you've read.*[3]

---

3   Rohn, Jim. "'Idaho Farm Boy Makes It to Beverly Hills.'" Speech, n.d.

Books have a way of not only educating us but gently making us aware of how much we don't know. And when we start noticing this, the wonder begins to return. We get curious about everything. A sense of mindfulness begins to show up in our life. We become a bit more conscious and aware.

You read a book about the environment and then you notice when you're about to throw away that plastic milk container and recycle it instead.

You've been reading a book about bees and walking from the car to your front door you stop and are in the moment long enough to notice the honeybee covered in pollen that has landed on a flower.

You read a book about the industrial age and while driving down the street you notice, with childlike amazement, the complex automobiles next to you.

Learning and reading shows us what we don't know, and when we can see that, our egos lessen, and that constant sense of amazement begins to return.

Did you know that the typical American watches three hours and 58 minutes of TV every day but only reads four books in twelve months?[4] Is it any wonder that we become cogs in a machine and forget our true nature of curiosity?

---

4   Ingraham, Christopher. "Screen Time Is Rising, Reading Is Falling, and It's Not Young People's Fault." The Washington Post. WP Company, June 21, 2019. https://www.washingtonpost.com/business/2019/06/21/screen-time-is-rising-reading-is-falling-its-not-young-peoples-fault/.

If you cannot tell, I have a deep-seated value and belief that reading is extremely important in transformation. But truly at the heart of it is this: by making it a habit to *educate* ourselves in any form, it stimulates more and more curiosity however it is you choose to do it.

I make it my goal to be curious and learn throughout the day with whatever I'm doing. I like to watch my youngest daughter who, at five, is still in a naturally curious stage of life. I aspire to be like her and try to imitate her wonder at the little things that surround us.

My wife, who is also a regular reader, makes it a practice to use YouTube to learn. She begins her day watching a Ted Talk or something else that is educational, inspirational, or spiritual, thus setting the tone for her day. Just last week I used YouTube to learn more about quantum physics, the basic tenants of Islam and how to install a new screen door because the wind destroyed ours. Podcasts are another great way to get into the minds of smart and enlightened people on absolutely any subject you could imagine.

Another place where a ton of learning takes place for me is through mentors. I can't remember where I read this or who said it to me, but I really like this standard, and I think it explains mentorship very well. At any stage in life you should be learning from someone who has advanced further than you, someone at the same stage as you, and helping someone who is where you once were.

The Perception of Value

We are unbelievably lucky right now. We are living in the information age. Knowledge has never been more prevalent or more convenient. Based on this fact, why doesn't everyone take advantage of it? I think one reason can be illustrated well in this story. As a salesman, I worked for a long time in telecommunications, assisting corporate customers with their voice, wide area network and information technology (IT) needs. One of the things we would do is offer to help a customer see where inefficiencies were located by auditing the services they were already using. This was to our benefit because in doing this our company could get an entire picture of the products they were using. It was also a benefit to the customer because they could either save money or reallocate their budget to be more efficient. What we noticed, though, is in offering this free service we ran into many of the same roadblocks from the customer that we always had. "I don't have time in my schedule right now." Or, "I'm happy with the services we have. I don't see the need," etc. So we tried an experiment that had very interesting results. We began offering the exact audit service with a price tag attached. We performed the same audits. The customer received the same information, and we received the same information to position ourselves as their vendor. Everything was **exactly** the same with the exception that the customer now had to *pay us* in order to give us what we wanted in the first place. That approach was far more successful, and our sales increased.

The perceived value was more because it was more difficult to obtain. It blew my mind.

To quote Jay Z: "Y'all think it's bougie, I'm like, it's fine. But I'm tryin' to give you a million dollars worth of game for $9.99."

While it's true that we're unbelievably lucky right now because we live in an age when knowledge has never been more convenient, that also may be why, as a culture, we aren't more interested in learning. Things that are easily obtained, for some reason, do not hold as much value to us as humans. The perceived value just isn't there. Even in our college and university educational system, a place where learning should be of utmost importance, the value is often perverted. How many of us focus on a degree instead of a true education? The value seems to be placed on what the degree will *accomplish* for us, instead of the real value of knowledge. If this weren't the case, the local library would be full of people and universities would be lowering costs immensely.

The purpose of this book isn't to be a solution to this perceived value problem for our culture regarding education. I write this only to point out the danger of this human trait. We have a choice where to place our value. We can choose to place that value on educating ourselves.

Our Opportunity in History

When we look at the great thinkers in history, we might think of the learners and individuals who were awake and who made huge impacts on the world. People like Leonardo

Da Vinci, Isaac Newton, Galileo, Socrates, Copernicus, Bach, Mozart, Charles Darwin, Seneca, Carl Jung, The Buddha, Jesus, Mohammed, Lao Tzu. Not even one had access to the information repository that today we carry in the palm of our hand. In fact, the odds against any one of them being born into the right circumstance to gain the correct education, find the right mentors, and do what they did were exponentially higher than what anyone today would face. Likely in history there have been numerous others just as talented and intelligent who simply didn't have the opportunity to learn what they needed to. Today, some of those minds that would have fallen by the wayside have a chance to bloom and it's because of this. I believe what we see today is an exponential growth of great minds. We see advancement beyond what I could have imagined as a child. My children, or at least my grandchildren, may have the opportunity to experience space travel. I will experience a car that drives itself. (Which I will absolutely own.) We can clone animals, we can manipulate genetic code to begin eliminating disease, in a matter of hours we can travel to any other place on the planet. We even stand at the precipice of artificial intelligence that will dwarf our own. In some ways it seems as though learning and advancement has outpaced our desire and ability to put it into a context that will not harm us as a species. Will we use all these wondrous advancements for the good of humanity? I believe this outpacing makes the need for developing the qualities discussed in the next few chapters even more important than for just personal growth. As a society, we need these qualities as we continue to advance.

Learning is a 'Big Block of Change'

Fifteen

Gratitude is a Superhero

As I've said several times already in this book, when I was "disfellowshipped" or shunned by the church and my family I was heartbroken, but today I am deeply grateful for it. It stands as an example in my mind of how the most terrible thing we could imagine can become something we are later grateful for. I tell this again to introduce why gratitude is important to me and how it changed my life.

It is because thankfulness is a building block of happiness, change, and transformation. It was the next Big Block of Change that I learned. Why do I say that? First, there is a lot of anecdotal evidence that this is true. Just look in your own memory for the last time someone genuinely thanked you for something. You didn't think to yourself, *That person is a dick!* On the contrary, it makes us feel good when someone is gracious. It also makes that person feel good. Think about the last time *you* genuinely thanked someone. How did you feel? How did you feel toward the person? Happy, content, warm? I believe this is because it's so hard to be engaged with our own ego and at the same time feel genuine thankfulness for someone or something. It's when we step away from ego that we are most in alignment with the Universe. *Gratitude is like a superhero when it comes to getting rid of ego.* When we are mentally and emotionally involved in gratitude, our attention is not inward. It's not our ego that's in control and when we get outside of our ego space, we glimpse a feeling of connectedness instead of isolation. It's the feeling of being a part of something bigger than ourselves rather than the center of our own attention. My mentor David Meltzer likes to say, "If you want to change your life, it's simple. Say thank you before you go to bed and when you wake up for 30 days." The evidence is not just anecdotal. Science has shown the same, most notably by Dr. Martin Seligman who is credited with being the "Father of Positive Psychology." Part of what he did was to back up Maslow's (think Maslow's hierarchy of needs) highly theoretical theories with real scientific studies. He is one of the most influential psychologists on the study of happiness and has done decades of research on the subject. He indicates that gratitude and other "strengths of the heart" are inherently linked to life satisfaction and happiness.

In a paper titled, "Positive Psychology Progress: Empirical Validation of Interventions," he and his coauthors wrote:

> *"... the definition of a character strength ... gratitude... is more robustly associated with life satisfaction than*

the more cerebral strengths such as curiosity and love of learning: (Park, Peterson, & Seligman, 2004). We find this pattern among adults and among youth, as well as longitudinal evidence that these 'heart' strengths foreshadow subsequent life satisfaction."[1]

And there are many others plus ongoing research that points this out. It's well accepted at this point in psychology that gratitude has a profound impact on our level of happiness.

Gratitude in Relationships

It's also a Big Block in happy *relationships.* Allow me to illustrate. When I was 19 and just out of high school, I started a small business cleaning grocery stores at night. I did a lot of the work myself but from time to time, I would also hire a friend or someone I knew to accompany me and help for a few weeks when things were busy. I wasn't able to pay them a lot but as a perk I would always try to buy snacks before and after work or breakfast once we were finished with work. In doing this, I noticed an interesting dynamic. The first few times we would go to breakfast after working all night I would buy the meal and the person was very thankful. He seemed surprised and happy at the gesture. But after 5 or 6 times, the thankfulness wore off and it came to be expected. When it did not happen, it seemed almost insulting.

1   Seligman, Martin E. P., Tracy A. Steen, Nansook Park, and Christopher Peterson. "Positive Psychology Progress: Empirical Validation of Interventions." *American Psychologist* 60, no. 5 (2005): 410–21. https://doi.org/10.1037/0003-066x.60.5.410.

I think this same dynamic can happen in almost any relationship or situation. When couples are first dating, they notice all the little things that are attractive about the other person. For example, my wife is incredibly creative and artistic. We were able to have very heartfelt conversations. I felt more open to discuss my true emotions than I ever had. She's kind-hearted. She loves animals, she's open minded to learning new concepts and she's beautiful! I was so grateful that I had found someone with those qualities and especially for the fact that she was attracted to me. (I attribute this to her low standards, or lack of good judgment.) But as time goes on, I begin to take things for granted. I notice the wet towel on the bed or the dishes that are in the sink. I notice that sometimes she farts so loud in her sleep it wakes me up. And things begin to look more and more mundane, bleak, more like a jail instead of a wonderful opportunity and partnership.

Work can be like this too. Can you remember how excited you were when you landed a new job? And how happy it made you feel? Yet as time passes, your boss seems a bit more overbearing. Janet, who sits in the cube next to you chews so loud, all you can think about is Nacho Cheese Doritos and her annoying personality. Janet starts to feel like the embodiment of every awful person you've ever met. She is unattractive and she always wears that perfume that gives you a headache. She can't stop talking about her cat, and you feel like screaming, "Get a fucking life Janet, I don't give a shit about your cat!"

Taking situations and people for granted is poisonous like that. What started as a creative, loving, beautiful man or woman that we're *thankful* to have in our lives has become a mess-making, closed-off, farting cellmate.

The kind-hearted, outgoing, sweet grandmotherly older woman in the cube next to us has become a mouth-breathing, Dorito-chomping, noisy cat freak! All because of a lack of gratitude. When we focus on and become thankful for the good qualities in others and remind ourselves to be grateful for them, it can't help but make us happier and more content. I know if I make it a practice when I'm angry to stop and try to think of something about a person that makes me thankful to have them in my life, I begin to cool off and become more content. It also becomes a lot easier to let the little annoyances go.

Use Gratitude to Control Your Inner Narrative

Is this just being Pollyanna-ish? Maybe. The bottom line is that it works. Using gratitude like this doesn't mean we become oblivious victims of life simply ignoring hurtful people and situations. We do what we can to improve things. Obviously, people should do their best to remove themselves from an abusive situation or relationship. But it does mean that *we control the narrative in our own minds*. Our perspective becomes one in which *we choose* to not be the victim of any further damage those things can cause by allowing it to control our level of happiness or how we react.

This also works for me when I think of past problems and things that were hurtful. It would be easy to look at childhood and focus on my mom's adoption of a mind-controlling religion that impeded emotional growth and restrained much of my life. Instead, I can focus on the good it brought. My mom used her religion the way I used drugs and alcohol. It's easy and it's numbing. But because of that, I can be grateful that she **didn't** use drugs or alcohol. I can be thankful for the times we had food from the church when she could not buy it for us. I can be thankful that I had at least some sort of morality taught to me. I can be thankful that she taught me the value of hard work and cleanliness and to look for the positive things that make a situation better. One of her favorite expressions was, "Poor and dirty aren't the same thing and they don't have to go together!"

As a result, our house was always spotless.

It would be easy to look at my father and focus on the fact that we bounced from one residence to another, that he was often absent and eventually was sent to prison. But instead, I am grateful that when he was home, he was affectionate and loving toward me. He was never physically or emotionally abusive to me. He was funny. He showed generosity to others with whatever little bit he had. If we only had a pot of beans to eat and someone showed up, they were invited to eat with us. I'm overwhelmingly thankful I learned those qualities from him.

I could choose to focus on and be bitter about losing my friends and family because of their choice to shun me. But instead, today I am wholly grateful for it. It gave my mind an opportunity to rest and heal away from the pressure and influence of mind control. For me, without gratitude none of that is possible and life would be extremely bleak.

Gratitude is an incredibly important 'Big Block of Change'.

Sixteen

You Are a Million Years of Recycling

Compassion is defined by the Merriam-Webster Dictionary as *"sympathetic consciousness of others' distress together with a desire to alleviate it."*[1]

I often bake things down to a 5-year-old level of understanding. One, because that's about how old I've acted for much of my life, and two, because by doing that I have been able to help my four daughters understand stuff. I came across this definition of compassion that works well for me.

Compassion is the emotion of feeling bad when something hurts someone else, and then it's followed by an action to help them. It is a feeling *and* an action. I'll explain with a story. While talking about compassion with Mabel my 5-year-old one morning, we spoke about watching for ways to show compassion that day in school. At the end of the day I asked her if she found any opportunities when she could do this. I was hoping she had not forgotten our conversation. Her face lit up. She practically ran across the room to talk to me about it. She said, "Today when I was in the lunch line a little boy fell down, and I was worried he was hurt. I felt really bad for him." I waited to find out if she had understood the *action* part of the quality. She continued, "So I helped him get up and gave him a hug." She was beaming!

First of all, that's a proud parenting moment. It felt wonderful to hear her tell me how she had acted with such kind compassion toward another human being.

Also, a couple of things struck me about this experience with her.

One, compassion isn't that hard to make a part of our lives every day. All we have to do is look around us. There are opportunities everywhere if we watch for them. Holding the door open for someone who has an armload. Wiping your feet when walking into a store, because you know that someone else must clean the floor. Letting someone in front of us in traffic. When Janet the woman sitting in the cubicle next to us looks like she's feeling down, taking the time to notice, and say something kind. Ask if there is any way to help. Or better yet just DO something that will help. Give the homeless person standing at the stoplight what you can. Sometimes just a sincere smile shared with the world is an act of compassion. By incorporating compassion into the small things, they become automatic in the bigger things.

The second thing that really stood out was that by helping that little boy who had fallen, not only had she made *him* feel a little better, she felt *incredible* doing it. It made her whole day to be able to see someone in need and be able to assist him. It was written in her every expression when she told me about it. Compassion pays back a hundredfold to what we expend. Isn't that what Jesus meant when he said, *there is more happiness in giving than in receiving.*[2] In my history, that principal was applied to the act of being generous with material things. Which is important but giving *stuff* only goes so far. The happiness of giving comes from the motive. When we genuinely want to *help* another person who is hurting, we show compassion, the quality that moves us the most and pays back the largest dividend in how it helps us develop.

This is one of the truths that is threaded through all the major spiritual traditions. Within Christianity we have the example of Jesus. The Bible says, *He felt pity for the sick and healed them.*[3]

Sikhism teaches compassion, or Daya, as one of the five fundamental qualities along with truth, contentment, humility, and love.

And The Dalai Lama, the religious and political leader of Tibetan Buddhists, humbly says this about compassion: *From my own limited experience, I have found that the greatest degree of inner tranquility comes from the development of love and compassion. The more we care for the happiness of others, the greater our own sense of well-being becomes. Cultivating a*

---

2   Acts 20:35. *The New Testament: New International Version.* Paulist Press, 1986.

3   Matthew 14:14. *The New Testament: New International Version.* Paulist Press, 1986.

close, warm-hearted feeling for others automatically puts the mind at ease. This helps remove whatever fears or insecurities we may have and gives us the strength to cope with any obstacles we encounter. It is the ultimate source of success in life.[4]

Simply put, a happy person is a person who has joy and contentment and compassion feeds both of these.

At the root of everything we seek are those two things. Every desire we have can be boiled down to looking for joy or contentment. All of our actions in some way are a healthy or unhealthy way of trying to gain joy and contentment.

The Science of Compassion

It's pretty well-known that the good parts of religion and spirituality promote compassion and altruism. And that's enough for many people. Saying to themselves in effect, *I know that this makes me feel good, and I know it serves a higher purpose, so I will do it.* That could be the end of the conversation. But when we take a look at the science of what is happening in our brain it becomes incredibly interesting.

Remember the effect fear has on our brain chemistry and how it limits our ability to successfully make changes? Its widely known that fear affects our parasympathetic nervous system with the release of cortisol and other hormones such as adrenalin. These are the chemicals that give us the *feeling* of fear. These chemicals cause an increase in heart

4   "Compassion and the Individual." The 14th Dalai Lama, August 22, 2020. https://www.dalailama.com/messages/compassion-and-human-values/compassion.

rate, alertness, and sweating. These things are needed when a fight or flight reaction is necessary, but they are also intrusive when we are trying to change behaviors because of the neural pathways they help to build. The more often those pathways are used, the more likely we will live in that state. Luckily, there are other chemicals involved that can assist us.

The interesting studies about this began with a hypothesis that females may not be as subject to the fight or flight reaction as males. That hypothesis was drawn because **all of** the research to date had been based on **male** subjects. The reasons behind this are many, as are the implications for our wives, mothers, and daughters when it comes to health and wellness, especially around pharmaceuticals. (For more information, check out the TED Talk by Alyson McGregor titled "Why Medicine Often Has Dangerous Side Effects for Women." I was shocked and dismayed by the information she shares.)

The research indicates that fear, which causes the release of cortisol and adrenaline, also has an *inhibiting* effect on oxytocin. Oxytocin is sometimes known as the "cuddle hormone" because it is released when people snuggle or bond socially. In the paper titled "Biobehavioral Responses to Stress in Females," the authors wrote the following:

"Oxytocin is a posterior pituitary hormone that is released to a broad array of stressors by both males and females. It is associated with parasympathetic (vagal) functioning,

suggesting a counterregulatory role in fear responses to stress.[5]

In other words, it seems that there is a tug of war that goes on. While fear can cause oxytocin (the cuddle/bonding/feel good hormone) levels to be inhibited by the release of cortisol, oxytocin levels, on the other hand, can have the *same effect in inhibiting cortisol* that causes us to feel fear. Suggesting that the more often we can activate the release of oxytocin the more adept we can become at overcoming fear. And guess what one of the best stimuli for releasing oxytocin in our brain is? Compassion and self-compassion!

Compassion seems to be the antidote to fear.

And since we've previously established that courage and overcoming fear is highly involved in our subject of transformation, compassion becomes doubly important for us when we set out to do so.

On a personal level, I believe that compassion is one of the greatest gifts that has ever been shown to me. I think of many times in my life when it was. When I think back on the people who have had the biggest impact, it is most often when they have showed compassion in some way.

One person stands out. His name was Peter Pintus. I met Peter in 2003 shortly after my father died. He was a pastoral counselor in one of the early drug treatments I went through. If there was ever a person who could have used circumstances to become cold and uncaring it was him. Peter was born in

---

5   "Biobehavioral Responses to Stress in Females: Tend-and-Befriend, Not Fight-or-Flight." *Foundations in Social Neuroscience*, 2002. https://doi.org/10.7551/mitpress/3077.003.0048.

1927 in Berlin, Germany, and was a concentration camp and holocaust survivor. Instead of becoming cold and uncaring he spent his life trying to help others. I am not qualified to tell Peter's story, only the profound effect he had on me as a person. When I was broken from alcoholism and addiction, and grieving the loss of my father, he showed kindness to me. Not only in words but just in his presence. He knew I was suffering and took the action of spending time simply sitting with me. He carried with him the very nature of compassion. What a wonderful example of the simple yet far-reaching effects of compassion. Even though it took me a number of years to finally understand the message the Universe was sending, I carried away from him the feeling of the kind of person I would like to be. It reminds me of something my wife talks about. She likens helping others to planting seeds. If we can just plant small seeds each day by the way we make people feel, it is enough. It is not up to us to make them grow. Many times, in fact we do not get to see them fully mature. But planting the seeds is our job. Peter died before I became clean and sober, so I never returned to tell him how he changed my life, but he planted the seeds for me. I think of him often with fondness because of his compassion and the time I was able to spend with him.

And there were other people in big and small ways that showed compassion. The compassion of someone giving my family food when I was a child stays with me.

The compassion of another family who gave my brother and I at least a few hours each week to understand what living without chaos looked like by having us over as guests, feeding us and treating us as if we had potential.

The compassion of Naomi, "the vitamin lady" from the church, that I poke fun at when writing about her, but who gave us a place to live and carried with her a compassionate nature.

The compassion my wife showed to me when, even though my addiction and behavior was causing her enormous hurt, helped me find help and a path. A compassion I will be forever grateful for.

When we examine our lives, most of us have been shown compassion over and over. What better way to give something back to the world than to practice it ourselves?

Finding Commonalities

Why, though, is it so hard sometimes to really feel compassion for other people? The answer to this question strikes to the center of what was involved for me when it came to waking up.

Growing up in a religion on the fringes of society automatically isolated us in many ways from other people. Our beliefs were different, and our actions were different in a manner that was very visible to the people around us. When it was time for a birthday party in the classroom, I sat in the hall. When other kids stood for "The Pledge of Allegiance," I didn't recite it. When they sang the national anthem, I didn't sing. Knocking on people's doors, going to the Kingdom Hall three times a week for services, not celebrating holidays, not making friends with people of different faiths, all those things made me feel *different. Separate* from the people around me. That feeling of separateness was celebrated. It made us special and unique in God's eyes. That feeling of separateness, although magnified for the purpose of mind control in my circumstance, is not unique. Our egos continuously cause us to feel separate from the people and world around us in normal everyday life. We separate ourselves by race, political affiliation, nationality, social status, and education level. Those feelings of separateness caused by our ego—the feelings of *I'm better than them, I'm worse than them, I'm different than them*—that's what stops compassion from freely flowing out of us.

Here are just a few examples of "separateness" I've had difficulty with, maybe you can relate.

It's been hard to hand money to the homeless person standing at a stoplight when I think his shoes are too nice. I think to myself, *He must be running some kind of a scam.*

It's difficult to listen compassionately to a friend when he is hurting because I judge the cause of the hurting is due to a stupid choice he made. "Uhh … Hey Pot, this is the Kettle … You're black!"

It's been hard to feel compassion for the guy on the side of the road with a flat tire when his bumper sticker carries the name of a politician I don't like. Seriously this happened to me and I drove right past.

I can see myself as separate in a million ways when my ego is involved. The way to overcome these is by focusing instead on commonalities. What do I have in common with the person instead of what is different? This became easily apparent to me when I started examining how much the same each of us actually are.

Our physiology is the same, we have almost the same makeup genetically as all other humans. Our genetic difference is miniscule at about 0.1 percent. On an atomic level, almost 99 percent of the mass of the human body is made up of the same six elements: oxygen, carbon, hydrogen, nitrogen, calcium, and phosphorus. Only about 0.85 percent is composed of another five elements: potassium, sulfur, sodium, chlorine, and magnesium. We share all of these. Yet sometimes we start thinking, this bit of oxygen, carbon, hydrogen, nitrogen, calcium, and phosphorus that I'm carrying around is better than or worse than that bit of oxygen, carbon, hydrogen, nitrogen, calcium, and phosphorus over there that that other person is carrying around. And while most of the cells in the human body regenerate every seven to 15 years, many of the particles that make up those cells have existed for millions of millennia. The hydrogen atoms in the human body were produced in the Big Bang, and the carbon, nitrogen and oxygen atoms were made from burning stars. *The very heavy elements in the body were made from exploding stars!* Pondering that causes me to become a bit humbler. To think I am made up of a bunch of stuff that has been recycled over and over and originated millions of years before I existed.

By thinking like this when I think of that homeless guy on the corner, who is almost identical to me in so many ways, except he is suffering in a way I am not. And his suffering is something I can help alleviate, even by a little. It isn't so hard to roll down my window and show him compassion.

We are all connected on a level so much deeper than what we see with our eyes. We are all the same in so many ways. When we are gone and the elements in our bodies have recycled into something or someone else, what truly will matter is how we treated one another and the legacy that we can leave on our planet and in our Universe.

I love how simple yet eloquently The Dalai Lama phrases it in *The Art of Happiness*. He says, *we are all 98 percent the same. All humans, all creatures, just want the same two things: to be free from fear and to be happy.*[6]

If we can look at it that way, race, politics, culture, nationality, social status, and education level all get insignificant and compassion becomes radically easy.

6   Lama, The Dalai, and Howard C. Cutler, M.D. *The Art of Happiness.* Easton Press, 1998.

Compassion changes our experience on a fundamental level as we continue to see ourselves more and more connected to others. Imagine the outcome when you walk into a room with a sense of openness, connectedness, and generosity along with a willingness to be vulnerable compared to walking into the same room feeling ill at ease, separate and with your defenses up. Either feeling can be true. We get back what we put out.

Compassion was the next 'Big Block of Change' that I learned.

Seventeen

Get Out of the Clown Car in Your Head

I'm hungry. I just ate. I should wait a while to eat again. I wish she would quiet down. Oh, that flower on TV is pretty. I wonder if it will rain tomorrow? Ugg, tomorrow is Monday, I don't want to go back to work. This shirt is too tight. I need a new belt. I really should make a trip to the mall. I hate going to the mall. Oh, look at that, I need to dust that table. Was that a car I heard? I wonder if someone's here? I like riding in cars. I should buy a new car. I'm hungry. I just ate, I should wait a while to eat again. Squirrel!

At any given moment that, or something like it, is going on in our minds. We like to think of our minds as logical and orderly, like a supercomputer of sorts. Nothing could be further from the truth! If you have ever tried to meditate and given up, this is why. Our brains are not orderly and tidy. They can be quite the opposite in fact. If you don't believe me, sit in a quiet room somewhere and try to stop thinking for just three minutes. Just 180 seconds without thinking. It should be easy right? After all, we can control our minds. What we find is the opposite. We are inundated in our waking hours with endless thinking. Experts from the National Science Foundation estimate we have between 2,100 to 3,500 thoughts per hour.[1] That is an incredible number! If our minds were a library, we certainly wouldn't go there to study. Our minds are more like busy train stations. This outrageous number of thoughts would not be so bad except our endless thinking is almost always repetitive. We may have between 50,000 and 80,000 thoughts in a day, but what happens is we have almost the same 50,000-80,000 thoughts the next day, and the day after that and the day after that. And this incessant thinking gets in our way. Let me illustrate. Have you ever been reading a book and after a few pages you realize you have absolutely no idea what you read? Or have you ever driven your car somewhere and upon arriving you think back and do not remember most of the drive because you were lost in thought? Have you ever tried to fall asleep at night and your mind just won't shut up? Have you ever had difficulty learning something new because your mind was elsewhere and no matter how hard you tried to concentrate you just couldn't seem to tune in? When we examine the number of thoughts and the repetitive nature of our thoughts, it's kind

1   Sasson, Remez. "Remez Sasson." Success Consciousness Blog. Accessed August 24, 2020. https://www.successconsciousness.com/blog/inner-peace/how-many-thoughts-does-your-mind-think-in-one-hour/.

of surprising that we get anything done at all. Not to mention are able to find even a tiny amount of peace.

I really like the analogy that Michael A. Singer uses in his book *The Untethered Soul: The Journey Beyond Yourself* when he describes it like *living with a roommate in our head.*[2] He suggests doing an exercise of imagining that little voice is actually outside of your mind and a different person who is speaking to you. The results of this exercise are funny and enlightening.

For me, the key to managing this clown car inside of my brain is a meditation practice. Of the few tools for transformation I have suggested, this, I believe, is one of the most important. It is like the glue that holds everything else together.

The excessive repetitive stream of thoughts that I could not shut off became maddening to me. Add to that a belief system and habits that were destructive, a self-centered lack of compassion as well as constant anxiety and fear, and my life became a train wreck. Meditation, something I was driven to out of desperation and just trying to keep my shit together, became an incredible transformative tool. I meditate each day to gently quiet my mind. It brings a clarity and calm to my existence. I learn faster, I perform at a higher level, I am more creative, I am calmer and more relaxed. I can be present in my life rather than always chasing something or running away from something. I can live in this moment

---

2   Singer, Michael A. The Untethered Soul: the Journey beyond Yourself. Oakland, CA: New Harbinger Publications, Inc., 2013.

of time. I don't have to be trapped on the hamster wheel of living in the past or the future. This is a wonderful feeling. Just finding out that there was a tool available to help was a huge relief to me when I began down this path.

The Case for Meditation – Why it Works

As I studied this tool of transformation, I wanted evidence as to why it seemed to be working for me. In looking for evidence it was interesting to look at high performers in our society. In his book *Tools of Titans* (a book that sits on the shelf next to my desk as a reference item for a multitude of subjects), author Tim Ferriss writes about the 200 or so top performers he has had the chance to interview on *The Tim Ferriss Show*. These are top performers in multiple categories, such as athletics, wealth, fitness, health and wisdom. It's fascinating to me that he says within this group of top performers, all from disparate disciplines, the most consistent pattern of similarity is a meditation or mindfulness practice.

Seriously, when we're talking about transformation and the tools we need to make change, what I just shared with you about top performers should be enough to put down this book and start a meditation practice of your own. But please, don't do that quite yet.

Since it was a form of meditation that I was using when things changed for me, it was the first tool of transformation I began to study. The information I found was nothing less than mind blowing. It's information that has been available from multiple sources for thousands of years within spiritual practices, but also information from modern science that helped explain what happens within the brain when someone uses a meditation practice. This information had been available to me all along. I had just somehow overlooked it.

My first steps in learning more about it took me to the writings of Buddhism. I was, at the time, very opposed to anything resembling Christianity but this spiritual practice was not offensive to me. I saw it as a personal improvement practice outside of religion. In reading books by the Dalai Lama such as *The Art of Happiness, The Book of Joy, Beyond Religion,* and *How to Practice,* I learned practical ways to meditate that also cultivated the qualities of compassion, gratitude and mindfulness. These began to transform my experience very quickly. However, even though meditation is a central practice of Buddhism, it is not unique to this spiritual practice. I went on to learn that the practice can be found in Taoism, Hinduism, Islam, Sikhism and Christianity. I found information on the Catholic mystics especially interesting to read. If you didn't know better, you'd think they were much like eastern philosophers. These different spiritual paths each indicated to me that meditation was a way to quiet the mind, become calm and connect with the Universe or the divine.

But it isn't just anecdotal evidence of top performers, religion, or spiritual ideology that show the value of meditation, today there's overwhelming scientific evidence showing the benefits of a regular meditation practice. It has been shown to lower blood pressure and boost our immune system. It can help with age-related memory loss and pain management. If you suffer from insomnia, it has been shown to be beneficial to reverse the effects. It also improves a wide range of emotional and mental challenges, such as the reduction of stress and anxiety. How is all of this possible, you may ask? One way is that through meditation, we become better acquainted with the function of our thoughts. By simply noticing our continuous stream of thoughts and setting them aside during times we are sitting, we change our awareness of our environment. A shift begins to take place and instead of the outside world dominating how we experience life, as if we are a passenger and not at the wheel, we begin to control the way the world interacts with us, through our intention, emotion and actions. The brain itself can be in effect "rewired" through a process called neuroplasticity.

You can find a simple explanation and a few examples of meditations that I have used at the end of this book. There are two important things to note when beginning. One, you aren't bad at meditation because your mind is active. As you sit in a place without distractions, remember that your mind will *not* be empty. That's not the point. The point is to notice when you have a thought, and gently nudge it aside each time it happens. That, in essence, is the whole of the practice. Two, try to practice for a few minutes each day. With repetition, the mind gradually quiets more and more. Daily consistency seems to be key.

Science, religion and philosophy all converge on this subject. A meditation practice can help us begin to better deal with our incessant thinking, open new neural pathways, and begin to utilize parts of our brain that we do not normally access while awake. For me personally, if all of the health benefits were nonexistent, it would not change the many reasons I have made this a practice. Each morning around 4 a.m. when I get out of bed, this tool allows me to get centered. It has become a refuge in my process of daily self-improvement. By sitting quietly and gently moving thoughts away as they come to mind, I have been able to gradually understand my mind a little more. When I am dealing with a challenge or trying to find the answer to a problem, it continues to surprise me that when I set the intention around the issue, and then sit in this way, the answer comes to me from the quiet of my mind.

My friend Adam Carroll, a well-known author, coach and public speaker calls this "The Inner Knower." I think that is a great description of it. Through it, I have become a kinder and more patient father, husband and friend, and each day I get to improve on that just a little more. It allows me space in my mind so that a much wider perspective can open. If you take only one thing away from the time you have spent here, take away the intention to incorporate a meditation practice in your life for a few minutes each day. It helps me personally stay aligned more closely with the Universe and connects me to the beauty that surrounds us, the beauty we are a part of, and the beauty every person has within.

Meditation is what holds together 'The Big Blocks of Change'

Eighteen

What Does it All Mean?

Today my life is radically different from what it once was. My thoughts that were once dominated by feelings of never being enough and a need to earn my place in this Universe, today have been replaced with peace. I no longer have to struggle with those fears and insecurities. Today my life is beautiful. Not because everything is perfect, or because I am perfect, but because now I accept that neither of those things really matters. With that came freedom. I'm no longer driven to live for later in a "perfect paradise" of the future, or to run away from a fear of Armageddon or even my own imperfections. Instead I see that we are all, each of us, beautifully imperfect. And out of that imperfection we get to experience incredible depths of compassion all around us.

Change begins with a little bit of courage. My little bit of courage was to say out loud to my wife, "I need help." The experience I had, led me to learning and reading, I absolutely needed to know more. More knowledge led to questioning my beliefs and deciding to design my own life's vision by realigning my values. Compassion and gratitude are the two values that have made the biggest impact. The daily practice of meditation helps me to do that, hopefully a little more each day. But the greatest part of this path is that it does not have an end point. There is always more to learn, new ways to show courage and deeper ways to develop good character. It's not a perfect path but it doesn't have to be. Each day I try to touch that place where change began for me and try to take actions that are in harmony with the better character I work to improve upon. The character of kindness, empathy, and less ego. The more I learn, it seems the less I know. For me personally, this came from a place of desperation. Sitting atop a picnic table broken and alone, contemplating suicide, I asked the Universe for help and I began a kind of meditation repeating a few phrases over and over.

I am calm, I am peace, I am love.

As I did that, my mind quieted. The incessant thinking was set aside for a few minutes. I happened upon a peaceful transcendent state. I finally heard the message the Universe was trying for so many years to give to me. *You have a place here.* I was given something I had longed for throughout my life: a bit of inner peace. I can't explain it and I can't put a face or a name on it. What was it? Was it the divine? Was it grace? Was it a glimpse of a reality we do not get to see most of the time? I wouldn't dream of trying to answer that question. But

I can tell my story of waking up and how it led to an incredible shift in my experience and changed my life. My biggest hope in sharing my story is that perhaps it can help you by reminding you when you need to hear it : *You are not alone, and you have a place here.*

I offer you my sincerest gratitude for allowing me to share this with you.

MEDITATIONS

What follows are some of the meditations that I have found to be helpful. You can find recorded guided versions of these on my website at www.wakingupthebook.com. As you consider these remember there is no wrong way to meditate. At times when my mind won't quiet it can feel discouraging. This happens for the most part when I have an expectation of what I want from the practice, instead of just allowing the experience to happen as it will. Regularity of the practice also alleviates much of this. Meditating shortly after waking up in the morning for 15 to 20 minutes and again in the evening for the same amount of time has been my practice. It seems that with meditation, like many things, consistency is key.

If you are dealing with deep emotional history, keep in mind that meditation can bring up thoughts and memories that feel overwhelming. None of this should ever take the place of help by a professional counselor or doctor. This is supposed to be a gentle process. Give yourself a break if you begin to feel overwhelmed, perhaps open your eyes, or consider a walking meditation that also involves movement of your body. If you are not overwhelmed, but feeling uneasy, consider sitting with your back to a wall rather than in the middle of a room. Meditation is not the place to push yourself, allow this process to become safe for you.

As you sit, especially at first, your mind will remain almost continually active. That is normal, you aren't "bad at meditation" because of this. In fact, it is the entire purpose of the practice. When you notice thinking, just gently nudge the thoughts to the side giving yourself permission to think about it later instead of now. By doing this over and over the mind gradually becomes quieter.

I like to begin each meditation with three short steps. You will see these three steps at the beginning of each of the meditations that follow.

1. After getting comfortably seated with good posture but not rigid, either on the ground with your legs crossed or in a chair with your hands comfortably in your lap, begin with deep easy breaths. Breathe in deeply through your nose holding it for a few seconds then exhaling through your mouth, exhaling just a little longer than the in breath. Breathing like this is linked to the parasympathetic nervous system, which influences our body's ability to relax and calm down. Breathe like this until you can feel the body begin to relax. You can count your breaths as you go, perhaps up to 10, then start over.

2. Then begin by considering for a few moments the many things to be grateful for today. My thoughts often go to my children and my wife. If I am outdoors, it's the sound of the birds or the wind. By actively engaging a feeling of gratitude the ego begins to lessen and puts our mind in a good frame to benefit from the practice.

3. Then, beginning at the top of your head, slowly scan down through each part of the body, making yourself

aware of how it feels. Are you carrying or feeling tension somewhere in particular? Notice this as you go but remember there isn't a right or wrong way to feel as you do this. It is simply an awareness exercise.

Mindful Breath Mediation

This meditation is a simple mindfulness exercise that has helped me understand the nature of my continuous thinking and to practice letting go of those thoughts. Modify it to suit your comfort. It's a basic exercise that can be returned to over and over.

After getting comfortably seated with good posture but not rigid, either on the ground with your legs crossed, or in a chair with your hands comfortably in your lap, begin with deep slow breaths. Breathe in deeply from your belly through your nose holding it for a few seconds then exhaling through your mouth, exhaling just a little longer than the in breath.

Breathe like this until you can feel the body begin to relax.

Now think of the many things to be grateful for today. Perhaps your family, your children, the very experience of living, the little things like the smell of a flower, the sound of someone laughing, the way someone special smiled at you. Your existence and place in this Universe. Place yourself in this thankful state of mind for a few moments.

Now beginning at the top of your head, slowly scan down through each part of the body, making yourself aware of how it feels. Are you carrying or feeling tension somewhere in particular? Notice this as you go but allow yourself to feel as you do. Remembering there is not a right or wrong way to feel.

And as you finish with this scan of your body, notice again your breath, counting as you go,

Breathing in-One

Breathing out-Two

Breathing in-Three

Breathing out-Four and so on.

When you become aware of the distraction of a thought, simply notice, and give yourself permission to nudge it aside to perhaps be considered later and return to the breath beginning again and counting each breath.

Relaxed breathing in deeply-One

Breathing out a little more than the in breath-Two

Breathing in-Three

Breathing out-Four

Continuing perhaps to the count of 10 and beginning again.

Do this for about five to seven minutes, moving thought aside each time it arises and returning to the breath.

After placing your attention on the breath for a little while, return to the awareness of your body, hearing sounds in the room, feeling the weight where you sit, any movement of air across your skin. And when you are ready, open your eyes allowing yourself to remain in this calm relaxed state for a few minutes before you finish the session.

Self-Compassion Healing Visualization / Meditation

This is a meditation I have used to assist in feeling more compassion for myself and also as an antidote to long held afflictive emotions.

In this visualization I personally have pictured myself as a small child and then beside that small child picturing myself as I am today, then I pick the child up holding onto him showing him the strength love and compassion he needed. By using this technique and applying it to your own individual experiences of times when you have felt alone, hurt, or afraid you can begin to heal.

A word of caution, this visualization can be quite emotional, so remember again, the practice of meditation should be gentle in nature not pushing us to extremes. If it becomes too much, return to a place of strength and love, letting it go until another time, or perhaps simply with the knowledge that you now know your experience and the depth of its effects a little better.

As always after getting comfortably seated with good posture but not rigid, either on the ground with your legs crossed, or in a chair with your hands comfortably in your lap, begin with deep slow breaths. Breathe in deeply from your belly through your nose holding it for a few seconds then exhaling through your mouth, exhaling just a little longer than the in breath.

Breathe like this until you can feel the body begin to relax. You can count your breaths as you go, perhaps up to 10.

Now think of the many things to be grateful for today. Perhaps your family, your children, the very experience of living, the little things like the smell of a flower, the sound of someone laughing, the way someone special smiled at you. Your existence and place in this Universe. Place yourself in this thankful state of mind for a few moments.

Now beginning at the top of your head, slowly scan down through each part of the body, making yourself aware of how it feels. Are you carrying or feeling tension somewhere in particular? Notice this as you go but allow yourself to feel as you do. Remembering there is not a right or wrong way to feel.

After these few relaxing moments bring to mind a time when you felt alone, or a time when someone should have helped you but did not, a time when the support you felt you needed was lacking. Perhaps when you were a child. Picture that child in your mind feeling compassion for what he or she felt. Perhaps you were scared, alone, hurt or confused. But now insert into the same scene yourself standing next to them, but as you are today. Perhaps you take their hand or wrap your arms around them giving them comfort and strength. In your own way tell him or her that things will be ok. You will help them through it. Help them heal.

And now for a few more moments sit holding that other self, giving them your strength and love and compassion.

Spend as much time doing this as you are comfortable spending. And then you gently let them go from your thoughts.

Now picture yourself with kindness and strength, whole, as you are today. Keep your mind on that whole complete loved and cared about feeling letting it fill you with warmth. Sit with this whole feeling for a few minutes.

As you return to the awareness of your body, hear sounds in the room, feel the weight where you sit, any movement of air across your skin. Allow the mind to go where it wishes for a few moments. And when you are ready open your eyes allowing yourself to remain in this calm relaxed state for a little while feeling loved and cared about.

Metta or Loving Kindness Meditation

Metta is a Pali word that means benevolence or loving kindness.[1] Metta or Loving Kindness meditation is a practice of bringing to mind first yourself and then several other people in your life and placing your thoughts of kindness and compassion upon them. It's not my belief that this meditation affects the other person directly in some way, but it has the effect of helping our thoughts, feelings and then our actions toward that person remain or move toward something positive. The impact is not the other person, it is us, our pattern of thinking and our state of mind.

As always after getting comfortably seated with good posture but not rigid, either on the ground with your legs crossed, or in a chair with your hands comfortably in your lap, begin with deep breaths. Breathe in deeply from your belly through your nose holding it for a few seconds then exhaling through your mouth, exhaling just a little longer than the in breath.

Breathe like this until you can feel the body begin to relax. You can count your breaths as you go, perhaps up to 10.

Now think of the many things to be grateful for today. Perhaps your family, your children, the very experience of living, the little things like the smell of a flower, the sound of someone laughing, the way someone special smiled at you. Your existence and place in this Universe. Place yourself in this thankful state of mind for a few moments.

Now beginning at the top of your head, slowly scan down through each part of the body, making yourself aware of how it feels. Are you carrying or feeling tension somewhere in particular? Notice this as you go but allow yourself to feel as you do. Remembering there is not a right or wrong way to feel.

Now in this relaxed state begin by saying the following to yourself

May I be filled with loving kindness and compassion

May I be well in my body and my mind

May I have peace

May I be safe and unthreatened

May I be at ease

Then we move on to someone else perhaps someone close to us that we care about, I often begin by thinking of my wife and daughters.

May she be filled with loving kindness and compassion

May she be well in my body and my mind

May she have peace

May she be safe and unthreatened

May she be at ease

Repeat this several times recalling several people you care about each in turn.

May she be filled with loving kindness and compassion

May she be well in body and my mind

May she have peace

May she be safe and unthreatened

May she be at ease

And now recall someone that you have difficulty with. Perhaps someone that you feel has wronged you in some way.

May that person be filled with loving kindness and compassion

May that person be well in body and my mind

May that person have peace

May that person be safe and unthreatened

May that person be at ease

And now letting that person go returning to yourself again.

May I be filled with loving kindness and compassion

May I be well in my body and my mind

May I have peace

May I be safe and unthreatened

May I be at ease

As you return to the awareness of your body, hear sounds in the room, feel the weight where you sit, any movement of air across your skin. Allow the mind to go where it wishes for a few moments. And when you are ready open your eyes allowing yourself to remain in this calm relaxed state for a little while feeling compassion and loving kindness for yourself and those around you.

About the author

Michael Gallagher is an author, public speaker and corporate coach who has spent half a lifetime studying transformation. He believes each person has unbelievable resources and untapped depths of compassion within them. He carries this belief into each engagement in his life. For some unknown reason he writes about himself in the third person and enjoys telling jokes in an English accent.

When he is not writing, speaking or coaching, he loves to spend time with his wife and four daughters. He lives in Winterset, Iowa.

If you have an interest in booking Michael for coaching or public speaking engagements, please contact him through his website www.michaelgallagherspeaks.com

Made in the USA
Monee, IL
18 September 2020

42947262R00111